First Love Yourself

A Journey to Unapologetic Self-Love

LATOYA JOHNSON

ISBN: 978-0-9975022-0-6

DEDICATION

This book is dedicated to my children, Quentin and Synaya. You are my first, my last, my everything.

ACKNOWLEDGEMENTS

I wish to thank the following people for their contributions to my inspiration and for being my personal cheerleaders during the creation of this book:

My mother Virginia Williams, you are my biggest supporter.

My aunt Michelle Lee-Barksdale, your role in my life has been paramount.

My dearest friends Regina Jackson, April Fraser, Lakeisha Brooks, and Michelle Blount for your authenticity and for always believing in me.

My mentor Bro. Bedford, thank you for your kind words, support and encouragement.

Thank you to my Journey to Self-Love Challenge community, and every Facebook, Twitter, and Periscope follower.

To anyone who purchased my affirmation CD or sowed a seed into financing this project, I also thank you.

I LOVE AND APPRECIATE ALL OF YOU!

CONTENTS

First Love Yourself: A Journey to Unapologetic Self-Love

FOREWORD

In American society, we're no strangers to making expressions of love to other people. Since we don't hear many messages about self- love, we end up unsteady in its practice —or not doing it at all. People with the wrong ideas about self-love may compare it to being selfish, but this couldn't be further from the truth.

My personal journey to self-love began in my childhood. I grew up in a family who seemed to have missed this vastly powerful information altogether. Even from a young age, I sensed there had to be something more than the continued strife I witnessed. Despite challenges, I've learned to love myself. I'm living a life I would have never expected. You can do the same, no matter your circumstance.

Have you ever sensed something, but been at a loss for words on how to explain it? A voice within has been sending subtle messages for you to love yourself, and waiting for you to respond. There is a message of love inside you, and the only requirement is that you listen.

Prepare to be enlightened and inspired. In this book, your dear sister Latoya is going to share a wealth of information on self-love— what it is and is not. This information will entertain, inform, and empower you. You'll learn how to nurture your mind and soul, meditate, discover your worth, and exercise faith and confidence. You won't be the same by the time you get to the end. You will have reprogrammed yourself into being a bona fide "F.L.Y" woman!

To maximize this experience, retreat to a quiet space where you can soak up the wisdom and truly process this great information. As you read, make a commitment to put what you're learning into practice, expand your perception of self, and evaluate your results along the way.

Stick with it. You'll be glad you did.

Xavier Ray Jefferson, Author and Blogger

PREFACE

As a success coach and mentor, I inspire people to become familiar with who they really are, fall in love with themselves, and maximize the value they bring to their families, communities, and the world. The process of developing into a woman who stands in her power and loves herself without apology is not immediate. It starts with acknowledging that you are struggling in the area of self-love.

The answer to most of the problems you've been experiencing with low self-confidence, strained relationships, slow personal development, and lack of momentum and drive to achieve your dreams and goals are all related. They're tied to the same root cause: a lack of self-love. Regardless of your relationship status, the past, or current situation, you are worthy of being loved, respected, and appreciated. It is up to you to decide to set your standards high and honor them, while also requiring others to do the same. The way you treat yourself and allow yourself to be treated by others is a direct reflection of how you feel about yourself. It's never too late to fortify the vision you have for yourself and embrace the powerful woman you were meant to be.

My goal is to help you find solutions to the problems you face within yourself, which will also remove barriers between you loving yourself, as well as provide tips on how to implement them. I want you to feel confident and reassured about who you are and discover the deeper connections in your family and intimate relationships. My desire is for you to explore the depths of love, purpose, and possibilities. It is time for you to experience a spiritual breakthrough, manifest abundance in your career or finances; and identify the changes you need to make that will give your life a sense of excitement and fulfillment.

Prepare to be enlightened with several practical steps that were created just for you; material that can help you find your path, discover the essence of your being and inspire you to build quality relationships with the people in your life. You are a step away from obtaining the power of self-awareness. Including the ability to analyze yourself, find proper answers to life's most personal questions, and gather the courage to live your life as you wish.

Although you may find these words of advice very simple, they are not magical solutions for everything. It is meant to inspire you and empower you to find solutions on your own.

After reading this book, you should be able to stand confidently in any situation, with pride and grace; you should be strong enough to overcome your obstacles and help others overcome theirs. You should be brave enough to speak the language of your heart, with the voice of your deepest desires. Your heart should hold joy for the future, and your soul should be full of hope. You should feel as if you have done something amazing in your life.

At some point, you recognized there was room for an elevated presence of self-love. More than likely, you chose to read this book because you realize that you are entitled to the same love you so willing give to others. This book will help you begin to recondition your thoughts and evaluate your behaviors. Thereby you will improve your self-image, increase your confidence, and cherish yourself more than you ever have before. This process will be an enlightening one of personal discovery. Searching the depths of your soul is never simple. However, accept that this process is challenging, but know that it is a fair price when you compare it to the increase it will bring to your experience of self-love. Before you get involved in the process, you should decide that you will be devoted to your personal progress. Your needs will come first, at least for a while, so you can be focused on things that really matter for your future development. Remember, committing to your personal growth and spiritual development does not make you selfish. It simply means you understand that before you love anyone else, you must know and love yourself.

The prelude to self-love is to evaluate the way you see yourself. If your thoughts about yourself are unpleasant, derogatory or self- defeating, then it is necessary for you to consciously focus on your value and shift the way you think about yourself. There are several ways to refine your thoughts and condition your mind with a new perception. A renewed mindset can happen differently for each person. Sometimes the shift can take place as a result of overwhelming experiences or encounters like it did in my case. My experiences were challenging, but I believe they were necessary for the evolution of who I became. I recently saw a quote by an unknown author that said, *"The woman I was yesterday introduced me to the woman I am today, which makes me very excited about meeting the woman I will become tomorrow."* What a fitting description for my personal outlook.

Although you may have had different experiences than me, I believe as women we share a common desire for healthy self-love, inner peace, and joy. All of these are necessary to cultivate a healthy love- affair with your authentic self. Today, I can proudly say I am filled with inner peace, authentic love, and joy. I can be honest and transparent about my past experiences, mistakes, and struggles as I inspire other women to achieve the fulfillment of unapologetic self-love.

Here is my story.

As a little girl and throughout my 20s, I struggled with low self- esteem. Feeling abandoned and inferior held me captive for a long time. My life's journey was sometimes dark, and I felt lost, unloved and confused. Fortunately, there was a light within me that I wasn't aware of for many years. Eventually, I found my light, but the journey wasn't easy.

At a young age, my mother was addicted to crack. Her addiction caused her to make poor and illogical choices. I'll never forget the day we were left alone with a friend of hers in the room she rented in a boarding house. This particular day, this friend of my mother's was intoxicated. A neighbor overheard her throwing up and coughing loudly, so she came to the door and asked if everything was alright. The sight of an overly intoxicated and discombobulated woman with two little children in her care was enough for our neighbor to call child protective services. I vaguely remember crying and holding hands with my brother as we were escorted into the back seat of a car. That day, my brother and I were put into foster care. We were four and six years old.

Within two years, we lived in four foster homes. We were shuffled around from place to place without time to form a bond or develop any sense of belonging. Foster homes are very unusual places, where a deep sadness collides with the inherent and sincere hope that lies within most children. Often we were deprived of care, compassion, and love. We weren't able to experience the innocence and excitement of what being a child. We were forced to grow up overnight. It was a childhood without any fairy tales, already touching the harsh skin of reality. We had each other, and this was the only consolation we had at that time. Still, there was a hope that we would find our way to happiness and normalcy.

After hearing that we were constantly being moved around in the foster care system, my mother pleaded with our caseworker to find a stable home for us. Shortly afterward, a woman opened her heart and home to a scared little girl and boy who was forced to take on the strength of a man. Her name was Kathleen Washington. She provided the first safe haven for two children who needed love and comfort more than they needed anything else in the world. She was our first trace of light. Regardless of all the past struggles, we were finally hopeful for a better future, thanks to Mrs. Washington. Although I was just a little girl, I realized I could conquer any obstacle; Mrs. Washington gave me this faith. However, the pain from the past left deep scars in my soul and my mind. I struggled with a lack of self- worth due to not feeling wanted, worthy, or loved throughout my childhood. . I began to tell myself things about myself that weren't true. I lived within the confines of the false limitations that I had conditioned myself to believe. Instead of focusing on my strengths and all the great things about myself, I focused on my weaknesses and the notion that I was not worthy of love because I was abandoned and had never met my father. Today, I consider those weaknesses and differences as strengths and opportunities. My story makes me unique, and I use it to inspire other women by disrupting the negative thoughts they replay in their mind to manipulate them into feeling defeated and worthless.

I also had a self-defeating story replaying in my subconscious. In school, I was teased and picked on for having dark skin, and I didn't feel like I fit in anywhere. My feelings towards my life and myself were much different than they are today—painfully different. I really wanted to be happy, feel good about myself, and find out who I was. The effects of being ostracized by my peers, and feeling displaced and abandoned caused more pain, struggles, and hopelessness. I was crippled by insecurities. I didn't think I was beautiful, and I always thought people were talking negatively about me.

Whenever I was alone, I wondered what it would be like to be popular and have a lot of friends. I sat on the bathroom floor looking into a little-broken mirror feeling out-casted and filled with sadness. I touched my hair as the tears flowed, hating how short it was. I'd look at my nose and think it was too big. Then I'd look at my forehead and play back how everyone said it was too wide. I thought being pretty meant having long straight hair and "perfect" features. I would get a long-sleeved shirt, put it on my head, and pretend it was my long beautiful hair. I used my imagination to alter my reality. I had never connected with the beauty, uniqueness, and value of who I was, so I escaped to a place where I didn't have to be myself. In my imagination, I didn't have to be that person I didn't know or love, didn't think was beautiful, and with whom I had no genuine connection.

It took me a long time to appreciate my beauty and honor my uniqueness. I wished I had more courage to be who I was, regardless of my childhood or what others said about me. But, if I hadn't had such experiences, I wouldn't be able to see things as I see them now. I wouldn't have had enough life experience to inspire other people.

As I matured and began the process of self-discovery and personal development, I started to look at my life and myself differently. When I was 14 years old, I read *Acts of Faith* by poet and author Iyanla Vanzant. Reading this book helped me to start seeing myself in a more positive and less judgmental way. It was the beginning of understanding my worth. I am grateful I found this book during my formative years; it helped me accept things and to shift my thoughts about life and myself to a more positive mindset. This book's influence on my life was paramount. I also learned to embrace the process of forgiveness, healing, and acceptance.

Many other books, people, and situations would also influence my womanhood and help shape my future. One particular day when I was 19 years old, I volunteered at a church to read books to a group of kids. I was reading *The Lion King,* and as I began reading, I was having an issue pronouncing some of the words. One of the teenagers in the volunteer group corrected me. I was humiliated! On my way home, I promised myself: *I would never be in a situation like this again where I couldn't pronounce a word, or I didn't know what a word meant.* From that day on, I began my quest of self-improvement, seeking knowledge and stretching myself mentally. I started reading more and enjoying the process of learning new things, which I had never done before. It was a time of very productive solitude, although I was actually never completely alone. New knowledge was my best friend. I finally felt as if I was getting closer and closer to something great.

Over the years, I embraced the process of learning myself. During this time, I heard the call of something greater for my life. Mark Twain said, *"The two most important days of your life are the day you were born and the day you figure out why."* This stage in my life of personal discovery was the beginning of another very life-changing transformation. I was more confident and empowered, and for the first time in my life, I felt important. What makes a person feel important? For me, it's the privilege to have a way to inspire other people. Using my voice as a vessel of hope for others means the world to me. It only required me to accept and nurture my gifts and strengths. The same thing is possible for you. Most of the things that can make your life more fulfilling and enjoyable are within your reach. Allow the lessons from this book to inspire you to discover more about yourself and tap into the love and joy you deeply desire.

For thousands of women in my Journey to Self-Love Facebook community, the process of personal discovery and increasing authentic love for self-started in August 2015 when they participated in an intense but fun exercise called the 30-Day Journey to Self-Love Challenge, with unique tasks, tips, enlightening questions, and games for each day. In addition to my advice and stories, you'll read about the Challenge. Some of the participants were kind and sent me their experiences with the program; they made a big step on their journey to self-love, and they are willing to inspire you as well. You will see how enjoyable this voyage can be.

Introduction

True Meaning of Self-Love

We often hear people use the term self-love, but rarely does anyone break down what it means. Self-love means to connect with yourself in a deep and spiritual way. It means to synchronize your God-given truth and spirituality with your character, behaviors, choices, and thoughts.

Self-love is not ego driven or vain; it is not an unhealthy preoccupation with yourself which disregards others. Self-love is different from the love you have for your loved ones. It's a tender, compassionate understanding and acceptance of yourself. Self-love is centered on a sense of knowing who you are and caring for yourself spiritually, intellectually, emotionally, and physically.

Who is a F.L.Y. Woman

Throughout this book, I will refer to the term F.L.Y. Woman. The acronym F.L.Y. means "First Love Yourself." A FLY Woman knows who she is, and loves herself passionately, authentically, and without apology. She radiates love and knows the importance of self-love. She is connected to her inner spirit and takes responsibility for her personal development and self-mastery. Self-awareness is the base of her personality.

A FLY Woman is committed to maximizing the value in her home with love, compassion, and understanding. She uses positive emotions to fight negativity and kind words to overpower low-level language. She reigns in her community through service and in the world through business and enterprise. She knows her worth. She knows her strengths. She knows her weaknesses, but she chooses not to be controlled by them; instead, she uses them as advantages. She knows her purpose, and she knows who she is. She embraces the Creator's plan for her life and makes decisions that propel her on the road to her defined destiny.

A FLY Woman is not perfect—she's perfectly imperfect—and she does not apologize for it. She knows how to accept everything that is part of her; her flaws are trademarks of her uniqueness. She embraces them, and she loves and accepts herself. She is walking in the direction of her Divine destiny, letting her heartbeat sync with the world.

A FLY Woman brings smiles to other people's lives. She brings them inspiration and motivation. She wakes up their inner strengths because she is empowered with the fortitude to do it. She sees things from a unique perspective; she considers every side of the situation and makes well-thought-out decisions. She is not a slave of prejudices; she is open to new people, places, and sensations. She is the embodiment of understanding. She is ready to help others, and she is not afraid to accept help if she needs it. She is emotional, caring and brave enough not to hide her feelings. She will make your day by just smiling and saying 'hello,' because her energy is light and natural. A FLY Woman is the epitome of self-love.

Chapter One
Recognizing a Lack of Self-Love

My Dearest Sister:

There is a process that God must take you through. It won't always feel comfortable, it will take time, and you will go through it alone; but know that it will be the most rewarding experience of your life. It's the process of learning to love yourself. Self- love means connecting with your beauty and the essence of who you are spiritually.

Self-love also means being responsible with your body, finances, emotions, and most importantly, what you allow to enter your mind -- no matter what it takes!

There isn't a person alive who can offer the fulfillment you will experience when you love yourself with passion and without apology. Whitney Houston said it best **"Learning to love yourself is the GREATEST love of all."**

Have you ever felt ill physically, but didn't know what was wrong exactly? Maybe you were nauseous and dizzy, or your body ached, or you felt more fatigued than usual. After visiting your physician, you found out you had the flu or some other illness. Did you know that having a lack of self-love also has symptoms? Some of these symptoms include insecurity, low self-esteem, and self-doubt. Fearfulness, entertaining toxic people, and indulging in self-sabotaging behaviors are also symptoms. You might have been feeling for a long time that something wasn't right; that something was standing between you and your goals. Perhaps even your personal relationships with family, friends, and coworkers.

Unlike most physical illnesses, you can't walk into a doctor's office and give them this list of symptoms and be expected to receive a diagnosis of not having self-love. Some women tend to persuade everyone that they are fine when in actuality they cannot bear to be in their skin. Those persuasive powers can work for or against you. Consciously, you may try to convince yourself that you are fine, but the lack of self-love is not something you can easily hide.

Symptoms of lacking love are easy to ignore. We pretend to be well put together, but that causes us to be distracted from our inner reality. It can be uncomfortable admitting you have a problem, but admittance and acceptance are always the first steps to changing. Do "normal" people dare to say they feel insecure or they don't have enough self-confidence? No. Nobody wants to be perceived as weak. Lack of self-love can be a serious problem for a woman who refuses to deal with it because the more she tries to hide it, the more it becomes apparent in different areas of her life.

Think back to a time when you found it difficult to believe in yourself and your abilities. You might have thought you didn't have enough faith. What about if you were in a verbally or physically abusive relationship? You may have thought you were just naïve and in love, and that's why you put up with it for so long. There is hope! Once you can identify an ailment, you are empowered to start the process of healing yourself from it. The fact that you are reading this book means you are ready to start the process of healing, repairing, and cultivating the relationship with yourself. I commend you. Most people won't show up to their rescue. Not you. You're ready to transition from having a lack of self-love to having an overflow of love and genuine confidence. Sometimes, it's best to start from a very early time in your life to begin rebuilding your armor of self-love.

Can you remember a time when you experienced rejection or when you began to believe some of the negative words spoken to you from your childhood or as a young adult? This step is a bit challenging because many of us have trouble with early memories. The trick pinpointing specific experiences and memories is to focus on the strongest emotions you have from your past. You don't have to remember every detail of your childhood disappointment (although it would be helpful), you only need to remember how it felt.

As you reminisce about your life trying to identify what striking incidences or traumatic experience depleted or stunted the development of self-love, you will most likely experience some heavy emotions as a result. Don't feel uncomfortable; I doubt there is anyone in the world that hasn't had some unpleasant, embarrassing, or painful experience. For you, there is no room for discomfort because your memories are the beginning of the bad times you have had, but also the beginning of a new, wonderful journey. Don't be afraid to face unsettling past experiences; after all, they have helped shape you into who you are.

I remember taking a walk through my neighborhood with a good friend a while ago. I'll call her Paula to protect her privacy. As we strolled through the neighborhood, Paula and I began discussing our childhoods. She shared with me how her mother would often have moments where she would become isolated, and her demeanor would be very cold and unwelcoming. When she and her siblings tried to interact with their mother, she would push them away and look at them in disgust. It was painful hearing her describe how the phases would escalate into rages and fits of verbal and physical abuse. Paula's mother would tell her she was too stupid to do anything with her life and that she was going to end up alone because she was too needy.

I watched Paula's facial expressions change, and her body language became guarded as she recalled the trauma she and her siblings endured. It was evident she hadn't completely dealt with her emotions, and the deep wounds from those words and experiences had etched into her spirit. As we continued walking, and she poured out her heart, I thought about a study that revealed for every negative or derogatory comment you hear about yourself; it takes 16 positive phrases to counter that one negative remark. Just like my friend Paula, it's difficult for many women to turn off the scenes and sounds from their childhood. They often play like a scary movie in their minds. It shows up in their life as a thief and robs them of their potential by keeping them bound to limited beliefs, which remain embedded in their subconscious. Paula later found out her mother was suffering from mental illness and severe depression, but that fact didn't make repairing the damage any easier.

This kind of damage cannot be erased or fixed, but over time, it can become easier to cope. That's why you should not delay confrontation with unresolved past experiences.

The most intimate part of your journey to self-love will be acknowledging and accepting the most vulnerable and delicate parts of who you are. The parts of yourself you might have buried for a long time because you felt they were not good enough to show the world. The feeling of not being good enough or developing a low self-worth might have started during childhood and then plagued you as a young adult. As you transitioned into a woman, this feeling also accompanied you. It's the uncomfortable place where brokenness resides within you—the place inside of you that can feel dark and alone—and it triggers thoughts that you lack something or not worthy of your heart's desires.

Maybe you've told yourself you aren't worthy of peace now because of some chaotic situation from your past. Perhaps you subconsciously believe you are not deserving of love. The good news is you don't have to be controlled by those negative experiences and limiting beliefs for the rest of your life. The key is to recognize when you began identifying yourself with negative labels, thoughts, and experiences. Whether it was what other people said about you, what they did to you or the moment you began to experience feelings of low self-worth from some seemingly unknown reason.

Take a moment to think back over the time when feelings of low self-worth and doubt began to show up in your thoughts. Make a decision now that you are willing to take the necessary steps to reverse the beliefs associated with those experiences. Do you remember details around what happened when you began to experience the thoughts that led you to have a poor self-image? What led to you feeling you were not worthy?

I'll never forget when self-sabotaging thoughts began to creep into my subconscious. When I was a little girl, I was often teased at school for being dark-skinned. As I walked down the halls, kids would yell mean things like "black sheep," and they would call me many other belittling names. I remember one boy saying as I walked past him in the hallway, "Oh, I thought you were an ink spot."

No one ever knew it, but when I got home some days, I would lock myself in the bathroom with my little broken mirror. I would sit on the floor, and I would cry. For almost an hour at a time, I would look into this little broken mirror at my short hair, dark skin, and my forehead, and I would think how ugly I was. I stared into the shattered mirror at a broken little girl who had no idea of her inner beauty, power, or greatness. Sadly, this was the time I began to allow other people's opinions of me to become my reality.

I want you to take a moment right now and think about your childhood. Think back to a time when you were a kid, and you heard someone say something negative to you or about you. What did they say? What factors led you to believe that what they were saying could be true? Can you remember how this experience made you feel? Whether you realize it or not, this was one of the many experiences that led to your thoughts and feelings of inadequacy. As I stated earlier, if you reflect deeply on your past, most importantly your childhood, you'll discover the root of when you began to feel self-doubt, lack of confidence, or inadequacy. Before this time, during your early childhood, you were free of insecurities, and all you wanted to do was play, have fun, and enjoy life. You were the happiest, and that is the purest and most beautiful part of who you were. The spirit of that playful child still lives within you. Your assignment now is to reconnect with this child-like spirit and start the process of getting reacquainted with the essence of who you are. If you don't know who you are, this is likely creating a deep-seated void within you.

One of the most profound steps in beginning the process of self-love is getting to know you. I am not talking about your official profile: name, profession, age, and social roles. I'm talking about discovering who you are at the core by asking yourself questions about your values, beliefs, and goals. There is something more in all of us. Something that lies beyond the basic, everyday roles society imposes on us.

I realize that not knowing who you are, can be a painful thought and for sure a very frightening one. It could be so unsettling, that people will do everything possible to defend their paradigms and their old beliefs. Why? Because the core function of our subconscious is to keep us from chaos, we associate this process with massive pain. Not knowing who you are, could be one of the most chaotic and painful realizations you will ever face.

However, the reward you will gain from passing this phase of development is tremendous. You will experience a level of freedom and peace that you might not have believed was possible before. All the false illusions that kept you bound will drop like dead weight. You will walk so much lighter, happier and relaxed through this world that your life today will feel like walking with a giant stone on your shoulder. It will be like you have been relieved of a heavy burden that you've been carrying since childhood.

Getting to know yourself is not something you can do in a blink, one afternoon or several weeks. Sometimes it is a lifelong process. Some people never end it. But you don't want to let your life go by without discovering your true nature, that's why you've picked up this book. Let me encourage you to remain diligent about the process of getting to know and love yourself.

Knowing yourself is the process of understanding you – the human being – on deeper levels than the surface. It is an unpredictable road that you must be willing to explore. It brings you face-to-face with your deep self-doubts and insecurities. It makes you take a serious look at the way you are living and evaluate your character. Be very careful on this path of self-discovery. Many people look to others to help them find out who they are. No one can assist you on this assignment. No one knows you better than you know yourself. Plus, if you ask someone for help, you will probably ask someone who is close to you. Close friends or relatives do not want to hurt you; therefore they will do everything to avoid telling you unpleasant truths. For example, if they see you as a person who doesn't have defined goals, maybe they will say you are relaxed and spontaneous and will keep quiet about how you should do something more productive. The problem is, when other people analyze you, their opinion is distorted not only by their interactions with you but by their previous experiences with other people as well. They might see you as a reflection of other people, or even a reflection of their own emotions, virtues, and shortcomings.

Essentially, you are the only person who can answer the profound question "who am I?" You are the only one who can be 100 percent sincere, open, and right. This book and the notes section throughout it will serve as a guide for you to your thoughts what enlightened you, but the intimate part of the process must be addressed only by you. During this process of self-discovery, you will be compelled to disassociate with certain low-level thoughts and behaviors that you might have picked up along the way.

Don't rush to change these poor traits. Raising the level of consciousness about who you are is a stepping-stone to the healthy habits and thoughts you will develop. This process of developing self-love will start with you being conscious of how you treat yourself. It is important that you also know your strengths, weaknesses and the characteristics you should develop to be the best version of you. Don't focus too much on those things you don't have. Instead, direct your attention to the most beautiful parts of who you are. Let your strengths define you and be sure to nurture your inner cheerleader. Also, be mindful not to compare yourself to other people. Comparing yourself is the surest way to diminish your self-image.

Here are a few steps for getting to know yourself:

Step One: Get to Know Your Personality.

The objective is to get to know your personality inside out, to know exactly how you are as a human being. Seek to understand what makes you react a certain way in life's myriad of situations. Ask yourself "Why did I do that?" and answer it. Who are you behind your name? What are your character traits? Who are you among friends? What about strangers? What persona do you portray to the outside world?

What are you really like on a good day as well as a bad day, in the face of a challenge or a great reward? How do you react to the world around you? While you're asking and answering, don't judge yourself. You're just information gathering.

Step Two: Uncover Your Core Values.

Your core values are the moral codes and principles you hold near and dear to your heart. When I work with my clients, one of my first requests before we get to our coaching sessions, is that they list their top eight core values. You probably have more than eight values, but the top eight are paramount in decision-making, influencing, persuading, conflict resolution, communication, and living your day-to-day life. Keep in mind; some of those values may have been instilled in you while you were young. Some may still serve you well and others may not. You have the power of choice. Keep what serves you and release what doesn't. Reflecting on your life and considering the person you want to become throughout the process of personal development will help you discover your core values.

Step Three: Get to Know Your Body:

How well do you know your body? Your breathing, abilities, limits of balance and your flexibility? You m ay know your body right now, but as you get older, it becomes quite an adventure keeping up with all the changes that take place. It can be a task knowing what it is capable or not capable of doing. The more you learn about your body, the more mysterious it will become and the more you push your body, the more it will surprise and intrigue you.

Have you ever said "my body can't do this" or "my body type won't do that" without even trying whatever it is your body can't do? Before you close the door to greater possibilities, take another look. Take the time to become truly intimate with the loveliest temple on earth, your own body. Perhaps you could try a new exercise and challenge your stamina. Or, consider how much rest is necessary for you to be functional and alert each day (which may or may not change over time).

A Universal Untruth

As a culture, we have certainly been misguided. The images we are constantly presented perpetuate a society which sets us up to despise how we look, compete with other people, and challenge our true being. Media is the main culprit, strategically and repeatedly placing contrived images of "ideal" beauty before us to get us to buy into their financially motivated agenda of stereotypical beauty. There is so much pressure to look a certain way, to have a high-level status, and to belittle other people through boasting and flaunting that it's a wonder we have so many insecure women out there.

There is no denying that media and outside influences can play a pivotal role in the collective spirit of low self-esteem.

Everything we allow to enter our minds through our eyes and ears gets housed in our subconscious and in our spirit. Whether we realize it or not, everything we take in mentally affects our decisions either consciously or subconsciously. When we are influenced to take on the identity, beliefs, and values of the world, we are shutting out our own beauty, truth, and personal evolution. It is up to us to choose how we see ourselves. Our own perception of self is critical, and that is the only opinion that should determine who we are, how we behave, and the level of love we embody.

In many cultures, little girls are taught to believe a handsome, rich, and powerful man will someday come and sweep them off their feet. Little girls watch Cinderella and Snow White, and they learn of other fairy tales, which express the notion that the great love we long for is out in the world. It is embodied in a knight in shining armor, or at the very least a man who is everything we ever wanted. Young ladies are taught to believe that it isn't until they find the perfect mate, have the perfect wedding, buy the best house, and have the cutest kids, that they will be fulfilled.

Needless to say, we have been bamboozled! The truth is the greatest love of all is inside of us. It's the affection we feel toward ourselves, not in an arrogant, self-centered way, but in a pure, healthy, and spiritual way. This type of love can be equated to the unconditional and unwavering love the Creator has for us. Our challenge is to detach ourselves from any conditioning, which leads us to believe a misguided and unhealthy.

Love yourself even when others criticize you.

You might have looked for a special type of love in your family, friends, and partners, but when you didn't find it, you were disappointed. You became upset and complained about not feeling loved. Embrace the notion that being and feeling loved begins and ends with you. Everything you've convinced yourself that had to come from other people is already planted deep within the fibers of who you are. All you have to do is nurture yourself and pour wholesome things into your mind and spirit.

If you want to experience more love in your life, you must treat yourself like someone you love. The great news is it doesn't matter how old you are; it's never too late to start loving yourself. You can start by doing kind things for yourself and let that be the foundation of a deeper, more fulfilling, and authentic affinity you express toward yourself on a regular basis. Make acts of kindness, love, and affection toward yourself a lifestyle. Be conscious of how you treat yourself compared to how you treat your family and friends. If you discover that you are overly concerned about the wellbeing of your family and friends, but not as concerned about your own, that's a signal to pay attention to and reflect.

Start with something small like making a personal vow to yourself. Walk over to the mirror and say, "Starting today, I am committed to being more loving to you." Make it a ritual to face yourself at least three times daily and declare that you love yourself. In the beginning, this approach might seem awkward and you might feel uncomfortable on the first few attempts. As you repeat the words daily, your mind will align with the words you speak. Along with other self-love rituals, you will begin to feel a deeper connection to your true self and your level of self-love will increase.

Love yourself even though you are not perfect.

Avoid taking non-constructive criticism to heart and letting it become your reality. It is understandable that we care about other people's opinions. It seems like we often have the wrong criteria related to it. It might happen that you get a negative comment from a person you barely know, a type of comment that is not in any way constructive, and you find that you cannot get it out of your head. That's an obstacle to self-love. When it comes to other people, focus on the constructive criticism of your closest friends and family. We cannot satisfy everyone's taste, so, focus on those who matter.

If you recognize that you haven't created the life you desire, don't allow yourself to make excuses. Whether the problem is the lack of self-love or something else, do not hesitate to solve it. Your goal of a better, happier life is worthy of dealing with every difficulty you might encounter in the process.

When I created the 30-day Journey to Self-Love Challenge, I had many different types of women in mind. I knew they all would experience the challenge differently. So, I focused on making it universal, considering all the things we have in common. Well, believe it or not, one of our common troubles is insecurity when it comes to personal changes. No matter how strong we are, we cannot avoid some kind of anxiety when we are facing such challenges. Or can we? While I did face a bit of anxiety and uncertainty when creating the challenge, I knew doing so we not about me, it was about each of you. So, we may not always be able to avoid some emotions that stir up, but we can certainly minimize the impact of such thoughts and direct our energy flow to a productive channel.

That is what the journey to unapologetic self-love is about: finding ways to face the ghosts of fear, initiate change, accept change, and love the change. It is also about learning how to deal with difficulties. If you focus, you will see that you are not the only one experiencing troubles in life, but you are surely the only one who can obtain control over how those circumstances impact you.

Journey to Self-Love Challenge Testimonial: H.N. Ward, Virgin Islands

The Journey to Self-Love Challenge is not just a game. It is profound and necessary first step in the process of loving yourself. This challenge has helped many women. I am thrilled when I read emails from the participants. H.N. Ward, one of the women most devoted to this program, says:

> *The Journey to Self-Love Challenge was 30 days of truth, emotions, and growth. Having to face me was one of the hardest things to do. Latoya made it easy with daily reminders, questions, and words to expand my thinking. The Journey to Self-Love Challenge was a life-changing experience. This challenge is perfect if you're ready to confront your fears and grow.*

Love Notes to Self

Love Notes to Self

_____

_____

_____

_____

_____

_____

_____

_____

_____

_____

_____

_____

_____

_____

_____

_____

_____

_____

Chapter Two
Alone but Not Lonely:
Self-Love and Relationships

My Dearest Sister:

You might be alone, but you should never feel lonely. There isn't a man alive who will know you more intimately than your maker; the Creator who has destined you for a Divine purpose. Your singleness is not a curse. It is a gift that's purpose is to reveal you to yourself so you can be cultivated and positioned as a queen who is prepared for her king. It's all a part of the plan.

It isn't anyone else's responsibility to make you happy. Only you can connect deeply with yourself in order to find the source of your happiness and peace. Having someone to share your life with is a wonderful experience, but you must also be content with the idea of being single. Tradition and culture have convinced you that being single is some sort of curse, or if you're single something must be wrong with you. Please do not take on the unconsciousness of this world.

You will never be able to genuinely love a partner until you wholeheartedly love yourself. Take this time to get to know, embrace, and accept the woman who lives within you. Give her your undivided attention. Create an atmosphere of love within yourself, home, and amongst everyone close to you. Work on mastering your thoughts, finances, and emotions. Build yourself up and create a life that's so wonderful for you having someone to share it with will only be a bonus. You are a masterpiece because you are a piece of the Master.

Society has a huge problem with the perception of being alone. By all social standards, being alone in any respect is perceived as somewhat taboo. They say you should have to have a lot of friends and you must go out often and meet new people, you must involve yourself in social networks. That implies that if you are alone, it means you're lonely. Of course, everyone expects you to have a partner. I believe being alone is a privilege of devoting time to your personal development, discovering the best of you and evolving on your journey to self-love.

Being alone is a sign of freedom and independence. It shows you are capable of coping with yourself and you don't have a problem being open and sincere about your life. It also shows you are ready to learn and devote yourself to your higher purpose. Of course, you should not neglect those dearest to you nor insist on extreme isolation, but you should never neglect your personal time either. Self-love still counts as love!

Many women are misinformed about the meanings of particular interactions with men. For example, just because a man lusts over you doesn't mean he values you. To value someone is to feel they deserve to be treated as important and worthy because of their usefulness. Many women can gain the attention of men. They receive gifts, compliments, and proposals for intimacy. The problem with this is once those experiences are over; there is no real value for the woman outside of what is superficial. In many cases, the woman becomes attached to the man, but he can walk away because he wasn't seeking her real value. Instead, he used superficial pleasures to create the illusion of something deeper.

We are more than our external appearance. People will never value who you are spiritually and authentically by judging your outer appearance alone. Furthermore, until we are completely connected to our own true essence, we will never be able to love ourselves wholeheartedly. In turn, we certainly will not be valued, honored, and loved by others with sincerity and authenticity.

I'm very familiar with this experience. In my early teens and twenties, I was always seeking validation from men. Because I was very shapely, I used this as a means to get superficial attention. Subconsciously, much of my self-worth was tied to the fact that I had a figure that could get attention. Being young and naive, I hadn't made the connection that the attention I got for my outer appearance had nothing at all to do with my self-worth. It took several years of personal development to understand the truth about who I was and to value myself enough not to allow my body to be misused in an attempt to look for the love and acceptance I believed I needed from others. It was a journey I wouldn't trade because it made me who I am.

Let's take a step back and talk about being content with your own company. Although having a lot of friends and contacts means a lot to every human being, why would occasional isolation be a bad thing? There is no need to feel guilty if you want to spend some time all by yourself without the noise and madness of modern life. Taking a break from feeling the pressure of fulfilling social norms is sometimes necessary. You don't need to exaggerate or avoid people all the time, but occasional solitude is a huge playground for people with a lively spirit. That gives you a chance to do nothing, but sit with and explore your thoughts. No one has the authority to tell that sitting in solitude is a boring or useless activity. It gives you time to gain clarity and reflect on important aspects of your life

I believe people are leery of staying alone because they are afraid of their own thoughts. FLY women should not have such problems because as often because we strive to be the masters of our minds, not the servants of it. Your mind is your strongest weapon, you and you can explore your most intimate thoughts, and choose to take the time to discard or enhance those them based on your personal self-love goals. You are free of any distractions and fully devoted to your own well-being. Enjoy the luxury of letting your thoughts flow naturally.

Alone, but not lonely, is my definition of perfect solitude. Your thoughts are the best company. Your ideas, plans, ambitions, beautiful memories and expectations can keep you calm and excited at the same time. If your situation is not so great at the moment, then solitude may very well be the best anecdote to put you in a state of deliberate focus so that concentrate on what you can do to change things. If you are about to make a big decision or solve a major problem, you can see things from a different perspective while you are alone. Sit back, relax, and do what you have to do. It will be much easier when you don't have other people's voices and opinions to filter through.

No man is an island they say, but you can surely take a short trip every once in a while and visit your island of solitude. Look at the sea of your mind, and enjoy the waves. Feel the wind of your life, and have a cocktail of good ideas. If there is a storm in your life, find a way to stay in balance with nature. Being alone with your most intimate thoughts will greatly contribute to your personal development.

Personal Development Through Solitude

When you read, watch a movie, or listen to music alone, you are highly focused. When you are on a movie date or listen to music in a crowded cafe, you don't have the luxury of clear thinking. Use this opportunity well; the book, movie, music and art that stimulate you can offer you higher doses of inspiration, joy, and sensations. That inspiration can encourage your thoughts to be like branches that go in various directions and form a beautiful tree that captivates your imagination.

Of course, reading plays a special role in our personal development too. When you read in a library, you take the risk of being distracted by things out of your control. Once you are alone with your book, you can focus on every sentence, get the message more clearly, and think about everything intensively.

Even if you don't read, watch, or listen to something, you can still make a huge impact on your own development while you are alone and quiet. Think about yourself. Think about who you are and who you want to be. Analyze your deepest desires and make plans. There is nobody to nag and bother you. You are truly free to shape your life.

How many times have you been in a situation and later thought of something you didn't say? When we are interacting with other people, we often cannot think fast and analyze the situation in the same moment. When we are alone, we have the luxury of distance. We can analyze people and situations as a whole. Once alone, spend your time thinking about something that made a huge impact on you, but you haven't taken the time to understand it fully. Looking at things from a different perspective, without distractions, has the power to change your perception.

This is a way to build your personality. The next time you find yourself in a similar situation, you can act more prudently. Sometimes experience alone is not enough—you know how people tend to repeat poor choices from the past. Experience plus time devoted to the experience really makes a difference. Solitude can help you understand other people, relationships, the world and how you interact with it.

Journey To Self-Love Testimonial:

Latoya Carter shared how the Journey to Self-Love Challenge helped her through one of her lowest points after a divorce:

Latoya "FLY WOMAN" Johnson's Journey to Self- Love Challenge literally changed my life. After my divorce, I was in a dark place emotionally. I had no semblance of self. I lacked confidence and self- love. I had already tried unsuccessfully at my own version of a journey of self-discovery. While I made progress on my own, my breakthrough began once I started this challenge. For thirty days, I received a timely email with valuable tips on a variety of helpful topics. The daily challenges had me engaged and eager to put forth the effort to experience a shift in my life. Through the featured word of the day, I was able to improve my vocabulary and elevate my language. By far my favorite part of the challenge was the thought provoking questions. These questions forced me to examine myself, my actions, and interactions with others. I was promoted to garner a deeper sense of self. Once I had this new, heightened self-awareness, I was able to accept myself, and ultimately love myself wholeheartedly and without apology.

Love Notes to Self

_____

_____

_____

_____

_____

_____

_____

_____

_____

_____

_____

_____

_____

_____

_____

_____

Love Notes to Self

_____

_____

_____

_____

_____

_____

_____

_____

_____

_____

_____

_____

_____

_____

_____

_____

Chapter Three
Toxic People: Not in Your Life

My Dearest Sister:

Recognize who's in your corner. When you're embarking on a new endeavor it's time to celebrate your accomplishments, look at the people who clap for you and recognize your hard work. Don't spend too much time discussing or focusing on the ones who ignore, discount, or belittle your accomplishments- they aren't important.

Support the people who support you! Stop crossing the ocean for people who wouldn't jump over a puddle for you. Show up excited and thrilled for your real cheerleaders. Share what they're doing, and always speak highly of them in the presence of others. Titles don't guarantee support, love, admiration, or loyalty will be given. A stranger will sometimes stick closer than your own mother. Count your blessings, not your burdens. Appreciate the love you get, and focus on giving it back.

"If you can't beat them, join them." You have probably heard that phrase countless times. I don't see why this phrase has become so popular because the words are misleading. Today, I cannot imagine letting people who are not good for me pull me onto their side. Have you ever felt as if you didn't know how to cope with certain people bringing negative energy to your life? With a bit of strong will and serious development of your emotional intelligence, you can change this. Consciously managing and controlling your emotions helps you build emotional intelligence, which is being aware of how you feel and being able to control how you express those feelings at all times. Emotional intelligence is an important part of self-love and self-mastery.

One of the first things that must be done to gain control of your emotions is to stop feeling like a victim. Don't blame others when you feel unhappy, confused, or unmotivated. Be accountable for your own feelings and actions. When you give other people control over your feelings, you are relinquishing your power. For instance, if you are easily offended by what other people say, it is your choice to either accept behavior and words you don't like or love yourself enough to decide not to allow the experience to affect you. The words and actions of other people do not have to be internalized. You have the power to choose the energy you operate in. Your discernment will guide you, and after several times of practicing this in full awareness, you will begin to operate in your own best interest.

The more you nurture self-love, the less likely you are to find yourself in situations where you're being taken advantage of or being misused by others. Your love for yourself won't allow it. Iyanla Vanzant once said, *"Emotions are neutral, they have no meaning except the meaning you give them. Emotions are simply energy in motion."* This quote implies that is it possible for you to choose happiness. It is not anyone else's responsibility to make you happy.

Being that your emotions are a direct response to your thoughts, logic would dictate the only thing that will bring about significant change in your feelings is to refine your thoughts. Have you ever tried positive thinking for one entire day? Have you ever decided for one entire day that you would not allow any person or circumstance to disrupt your peace? If not, I want to challenge you to be positive and peaceful for an entire day.

Now, as you experiment with this idea, you'll realize it isn't easy to do. You know the voice inside of your head, which creates internal conversations, mental movies about past events, and random chatter? Well, this voice and those mental images have no power other than the power you give them. Here is a great poem by Ritu Ghatourey, a writer from India:

> Your mind is a garden
> and your thoughts are the seeds;
> you can either grow flowers
> or you can grow weeds.

This poem is a reminder that you have power over your thoughts, and no negative thought can dwell in your mind without your permission. The key is to let each thought—the positive ones and the negative ones—pass without thinking about it too long. Doing so will also help you to think in the moment.

It is also critical to monitor the images and conversations you allow yourself to be exposed to. When your goal is to be positive, peaceful, and exercise your power, it is important for you to stay tuned into positive images, people, conversations, and behaviors. The people you talk to can have a large bearing on your subconscious mind.

Here's an example:

My godmother is very organized and meticulous, whereas I am the total opposite. Often when I speak with her, she talks about how she has planned every detail of whatever she's engaged in or how she wants everything to operate in excellence and in order. Even when she tells a story, she includes every detail, and she speaks very precisely and in a well-thought-out fashion. When I get off the phone with her, I suddenly feel like cleaning up or organizing something in my own space. In this case, her conversation and energy have a positive influence.

As with those who positively impact your subconscious mind, there are other people you will converse with whose energy will have the opposite effect. When you're done talking to them, you might feel drained, sluggish or discouraged. Until now, you might not have made the connection between their toxic energy rubbing off on you and occupying space in your subconscious. These are the relationships you want to evaluate and ask yourself: What is this relationship doing to me? Does it inspire me or help me to progress? Does it bring out the best in me? Answering these questions truthfully will guide you to make healthy relationship choices. Always remember you have authority to remove yourself from toxic relationships that do not foster peace and growth.

One major characteristic of water is that it seeks its own level. As humans, we also seek our own level. If you put 100 random people in a room, before long like minds will be drawn to one another. That's how powerful influence and energy are.

It's difficult to see the picture when you're in the frame. For instance, you might have given advice to a friend who was in a certain situation. Because you were on the outside, you were able to see that your friends' energy may have been contributing to the unfavorable situation they were experiencing. If you want to change the energy you attract, then you must first change the energy you carry. By being conscious of your energy, you will more carefully evaluate the people in your life, the people you attract, and those to whom you are attracted.

That's not to say you are better than any person, but as you evolve, you will no longer attract or be attracted to certain activities, conversations, and behaviors. Think about the disciplines, behaviors, and new philosophies you can adopt to keep yourself in alignment with what and who you want to attract into your life. Discernment developed through your experiences will enable you to choose your associations wisely. Remember, everyone you meet or connect with is not meant to be permanent in your life. Keep your circle small. Engage with new people, but be mindful of the energy they bring.

Make a conscious effort to surround yourself with people who are happy, loving, easy-going, and compassionate. You will notice that when you speak to them or when you are in their company. On the other hand, your energy level is high, and you feel motivated, inspired, or encouraged. Be wary of people who are always frustrated, stressed-out, angry, or negative. These people are likely to influence your positive energy with their negativity.

Toxic people challenge our emotional development of staying calm and balanced. Their influence can often be contagious. Sometimes they don't seem dangerous or malicious, but they still have a bad influence on your mood. Bit by bit they can have a serious impact on your normal mood and attitudes. Save yourself before it is too late. Pinpoint them and decide whether it would be healthy to distance yourself from them. If it is a spouse, co-worker, or someone you cannot easily avoid, build up an armor of positive, so the negative will have less impact and ensure you recharge around positive people.

You don't have to argue with them or create additional tension. You just need to isolate your potential of well-being from the danger of their toxicity. You do not disown them; you simply send them away to find the course of their own. Such people are often unhappy, and they are often the ones who need help with interpersonal development. Although you may want to help them, maybe you should wait a bit, at least until you are done with your own personal pursuit of balance. Further, them needing help and seeking help are two different things. If you're still working on you and try to help someone not seeking help, chances are, you're setting yourself up for failure. They can impose obstacles in your way that can derail you from your self-love and journey to personal mastery.

Focus on good people instead of the ones who bring out the best in you. Appreciate their kind words, love, and respect. Get infected by their optimism and positive vibe. To become more capable of bonding with amazing people, you will have to cut the complicated relationships with toxic people in your life first. Here are some easy steps you can use to help.

Step One: Identify Toxic People in Your Life

Don't be afraid, to be honest about who in your life is not bringing healthy vibes. Your personal peace is more important than cherishing relationships that don't do you any good. You may find this difficult; after all, there are probably some difficult people in your life who are dear to you. In the name of long friendships and connections, some of us will keep quiet about things that bother us. This is a big mistake. Do not be afraid to be true to yourself. Ignoring problems leads to more problems.

Identifying people who perpetuate trouble, anxiety, and bad moods is a logical first step to a better life with more freedom. Take a moment and inventory the people in your life. Who causes you to feel drained and exasperated? You certainly don't want to continue allowing them to disturb your peace. So go ahead and name those individuals specifically and make a decision.

Step Two: Set the Right Boundaries

Once you admit who those toxic people are, you might consider building a mental shield around yourself. If they are not too serious of a threat, build a shield around you. Doing so should let them know that they can't have a negative impact on your life anymore. Be discreet, kind, and don't lose your dignity. But also be proud of your ability to choose your peace of mind over their presence.

For example, if a nagging acquaintance calls you for a lunch date, skip it. It's important to guard your spirit from toxic energy while you are on your journey of personal discovery. People do change. One day you will dine with them without hesitation, but for now, try to eliminate meetings with anyone who brings stress to you. If you feel strong enough to express your emotions in a more direct manner, you should do it. Let them know they cannot pour their counterproductive energy on you. Cherish your optimism, and if they don't respect it, they shouldn't be around you.

Some of these toxic people may carry negativity unconsciously. Therefore, your criticism could be either constructive or offensive to them. Find comfort in knowing, you are not responsible for their responses; this is why you should be careful while setting your boundaries. Do not get into conflict intentionally. Try to be fair and reasonable. If your boundaries make some people uncomfortable, don't feel obligated to apologize. Regarding self-love, it is necessary to honor your personal standards. Be careful not to give into the pressure of accepting what you don't want in your life.

Step Three: Never Ignore Toxic People around You

I've heard a lot of people say we should ignore annoying, toxic people. How can we do it if they are constantly around us? These people could be a problem for everyone who spends time with them. However, sometimes it's possible to raise their consciousness and tell the negative person there are other moods besides grumpy? Perhaps encourage them to see beauty in something or to consider all that they have to be grateful for. Don't be surprised if receive push back, especially if they don't realize how toxic they are; you've done more for them than anyone else, you've planted a seed.

Imagine you have just had breakfast and left a few dishes in the sink. Suppose you did the same after lunch, snack, and dinner. Would you have a pile of dishes? That would be a mess. The more you delay the dish washing, the more difficult it seems to motivate yourself to wash them. Emotions are even worse than dishes. Don't let them pile up; the consequences are more than messy. If you see someone is negative, don't delay to position yourself as safe from this person's influence as possible. Either actively isolate yourself or speak up. Your spirit will be grateful, and it will compensate you with a calmer stress-free day Limiting your time around toxic people may be one of the most difficult tasks, but it is also the most necessary step on your journey to self-love. Whatever your motivation is that encouraged you to read this book, your weapon that will keep you track should be your courage.

Ignoring problems is always the worse choice you could make. Dealing with them is an attribute of a real FLY woman.

Step Four: Beat Toxicity with Your Positive Energy

As Phyllis Diller said, "A smile is a curve that sets everything straight." Being positive is the simplest strategy to combat pessimistic tendencies. I believe you have enough optimism to fuel the beautiful thoughts in your mind to become immune to toxicity; you have to believe it too.

Now, don't be confused; simply being positive around negative people is not ignoring their negativity. It is the opposite. You are actively trying to bring beauty to their general mood. You may even manage to inspire toxic people to get into a more comfortable mode. It is a great challenge. Nothing kills a bad atmosphere like a dose of kindness and laughter. You know you have it in you. Wake it up and change the energy flow in a more favorable direction. Add a bit of humor to their long, nagging sentences. Help them realize that it's okay to tap into joy, laughter, and happiness.

Journey to Self-Love Challenge Testimonial:
Carla Tribble, Maryland

Getting rid of toxic people requires building a strong personality and the audacity to say what you feel. One of the many women who took the Journey to Self-Love Challenge, Carla, was encountering many troubles in her relationships with other people.

Sound familiar?

Carla overcame many of her troubles through this challenge. Her experience may have been intense, but it was sobering as well. Sometimes we realize the reason for our bad communication and complicated relationships with others lies within us. If this is the problem, we should not avoid facing it. Realizing we are doing something unhealthy is a great first step. It means we have the consciousness to change it.

It can turn out that all those toxic people can be a secondary problem, while the bigger problem is within your power to change. If this is the case, if you feel like you could improve yourself to achieve better treatment of other people, you will probably enjoy Carla's story. Pay attention; she is proof that such problems are not insurmountable. Personal change is possible and necessary. Once you detect the problem within your own mind, you can fix it by relying on the strongest characteristics to avoid many unfavorable circumstances. Here is how Carla did it:

"Before I accepted the 30-Day Journey to Self-Love Challenge, I was insecure and completely out of touch with who I was or what I really wanted. I'd sacrificed everything about me effort to please others. The Journey to Self- Love Challenge helped me to love myself more. Like a butterfly coming out of a cold, dark cocoon, I had been hiding my whole life. Now I'm beginning to choose how I want to feel. I realized how I was treating myself showed others how to treat me. The third day of the challenge I vowed to put myself first and be kind, loving, and generous to myself. Out of self-respect and desperately needing a fresh start, I walked away from the old me. My journey to self-love also showed me the importance of prioritizing my dreams and making an effort to do things that inspire me and lift me up. Also saying no to things I don't agree with or that don't fit in my plans. I found the courage to try new things that I've always wanted to experience. Gifting myself forgiveness and accepting myself for all my beautiful and imperfect quirks and qualities. Once I completed the challenge, I was able to flow freely without judgment or pretense. I was nourished and inspired to encourage other women to live a happier and more vibrant life."

Love Notes to Self

_____

_____

_____

_____

_____

_____

_____

_____

_____

_____

_____

_____

_____

_____

Love Notes to Self

_____

_____

_____

_____

_____

_____

_____

_____

_____

_____

_____

_____

_____

_____

_____

Chapter Four
Leave the Past Behind You

My Dearest Sister:

No one has the authority to use your past to make you feel naked and exposed. When your past creeps up in an attempt to make you feel ashamed or vulnerable; stand up to it and snatch all of its lessons, but leave the experience right where it belongs, behind you!

*Every person on earth has done something in their life that didn't represent the best and the highest within them. Despite what you have done; no matter how awful or deplorable you might think it is there is still room for you at the table where forgiveness, love, and restoration are being served. Your silverware will be grace and mercy, and redemption will be your dessert. Once you are full, you will begin to share your testimony from the perspective of victor and not victim. Adopt the words of the great poet Maya Angelou, **"I can be changed by what happens to me but I refuse to be reduced by it."***

Self-love and self-appreciation require you to be open for whatever may come your way. Mistakes are our occasional guests. Sometimes it is impossible to avoid them, and trying to avoid them might not be the right solution as it will deprive you of all the gifts mistakes bring such as lessons learned, personal growth and strength to name a few.

The key to coping with past mistakes is confronting them. It's not like when you have to confront someone you dislike or someone who bothers you. It is a confrontation with your past choices and behavior. This is why the process often seems like you're running in circles. We go on and on with our endless self-accusing and self-pity. We find irrational reasons to make ourselves feel guilty when we want to feel better at the same time.

While we cry about those past days and the natural human mistakes, the Creator has already forgiven us. We are stronger than our sadness. All we need to do is embrace the spirit of forgiveness and continue our lives without any fear. If a mistake comes up again, you can always get back on track. You are resilient and courageous. Many times before, you have proven that you have comeback power. This time will be no different. Your present is not a moment after a hurtful past but it is a glorious time before a wondrous future. Don't let mistakes from your past diminish your faith and hope for future opportunities. You are no longer that misguided person who acted unconsciously. You now have greater discernment. You are wiser and more intuitive than you were before you picked up this book.

My objective is to encourage and inspire you to believe you can overcome any past situation. I am not trying to promise you a life filled with all sunshine and roses. When you do reach the point where you've overcome some mishaps of the past, you will be more equipped when another mistake happens. Cheer yourself on with "I've come back before; I'll come back again." Trust me. I know what it feels like to be trapped in the dark valleys of our past. For years, I was feeling less than worthy because I thought my past defined me. Consequently, this is a misguided thought that has no place in our minds. You are not your past. You are full of plans and ambitions, energy, motivation, and aspirations. The future is full of endless possibilities. Disassociate from the darkness of your mistakes and connect with the brightness that the present and future experiences behold. I know, it's easy to write such things, but how does this work in reality? I've used my personal memories and experiences to come up with some basic steps meant to make things easier for you. I hope some of these will invoke positive energy and relieve any pain that you might still be experiencing.

Step One: Accept Your Mistakes

I've already mentioned this, and I will reiterate it many times: acceptance is the key to developing mental and emotional mind mastery. When you accept things as they are, you can come up with a way to change them. It's the same thing with your past. We don't have a time- machine to fix the parts of our personal history that we don't like. This is more of a reason why we need to be brave and confront them. Don't be afraid to admit that your past was not perfect. Stand in front of a mirror and tell yourself "I made a mistake; *I am not the mistake.*

Define your mistake in details. Let the emotions flow naturally and without judgment and don't let the negative ones haunt you. Take advantage of your desire to make things right and balance your emotions. Be aware of possible feelings of shame. You will feel compelled to escape from it, but ignoring it is not the right solution; in fact, it may be one of the reasons you're where you are now. "If you do what you've always done, you'll get what you've always gotten" (Jim Rohn). Your escape comes when you have accepted everything that comes with it. After you are sure you don't have a problem admitting everything, from the behavior to the consequences of the behavior, it is important to accept that there is a chance to make things right again.

Step Two: Accept That Your Past Doesn't Make You a Bad Person

If events from your past still make you feel bad, you need to know those past events are only one part of your life's experience. One part by itself doesn't make a whole. And it doesn't have to dictate your mood and feelings. There is no perfect human being. You may believe there are flawless people; indeed, some people seem like they never make mistakes. The reality is they make mistakes, just like you and me. The difference is they cope with their mistakes well. They don't let their mistakes ruin their days. They simply know those past torments are not something they want to feel forever. You can learn from such people—I know I did—and become free of negative obsessions. I didn't use the word obsession lightly. Negativity is addicting and contagious, and the word obsession implies a lack of self-control. Take back control.

Here is an exercise to help you in the area of releasing negative experiences from the past. Start with one sheet of paper. Take two different pens, one in black and the other in any cheerful color. Randomly write the good and bad things you have done in your past. Write what you consider bad in black. For everything written in black, write three things written in bright color. Let the cheerful color prevail. Remind yourself that your past wasn't pointless, and give yourself credit for all the great things you have done.

Step Three: Learn from Your Past

Those nasty ghosts of the past can always teach you a valuable lesson. Listen to what they have to say, take notes, and be their best student. Although you may feel uncomfortable getting back to the past for any reason, you shouldn't skip the golden opportunity of learning from your experience. Make every experience count. If it's all done, you should be able to overcome the fear and enjoy analyzing the situation. When you're experiencing first hand, there is an emotional reference point that is more likely to stick with you. Learning from our own mistakes is not as easy as learning from other people's bad decisions. It is more challenging because it affected us personally, and because of that, it's more interesting, and, most importantly, more influential. The experiences will teach you, and you will likely remember them forever.

Here is another helpful exercise. Take a nice little notebook and writing your mistakes there. It doesn't have to be listed chronologically. Put life lessons next to mistakes. Make it simple. For example:

Mistake: I couldn't meet my deadlines. Life lesson: Be more organized.

Compare your mistakes. Do you repeat some of them? Was there a chance to avoid some of them? Be your own teacher and learn without any pressure but with the objective of making peace with your past choices.

Step Four: Do Something Charitable or Kind

Some people feel they can replace mistakes with good deeds. I don't think past mistakes can or should be erased, replaced, or destroyed. But I do believe good deeds are welcomed if they are going to relieve your troubles. Challenge yourself to do something nice for yourself or others. If your mistakes and past pain are related to a particular person, do something special for this person. Your past must be accepted as is. However, you can balance the regret by doing something nice. Go ahead—you will be a step closer to forgiving yourself. The fulfillment of a kind act is more sincere than the unintentional bad things you have done in the past. Allow this feeling to dwell. Let it remind you of your goodness, positive energy potential, and genuine spirit. Do things that bring out the best in you.

Step Five: Put Your Past in Perspective

To make things right and become ready to forgive yourself, you need to make a few changes regarding your perspective. If you are coping with the problem of haunting past memories, your life's timeline will be complicated. Normal timeline, of course, implies chronological past, present, and future. When one is facing past problems, those problems are mixing in with their present and may affect their future if not addressed What we have is past, present-past, and future-past. It is reliving the past in circles.

There are many ways to solve this time-machine knot. One of them is to remember the many situations that made you feel good. Come up with things that make you feel good at this particular time in your life. Brainstorm ideas you want to implement in your future, things that should bring you positive feelings and outcomes. Now, draw a timeline and put all of the above together, chronologically.

Don't forget your ghosts of the past; put them in their place, right where they belong because you do want to acknowledge them. You are not trying to deny them. The idea is to see how many better things you have done, how many more positive things you can do now, and how many great deeds you will do in days to come. By drawing your attention to the nice things that wake up pure joy in you, your past mistakes should seem like tiny dots. This little game can help you realize your past doesn't define you.

There is so much more to you than a few poor choices or misguided past behaviors. You have kindness, gentleness, and compassion within you. Embrace that, and give your soul a chance to be free from repression.

Step Six: Do Physically Pleasant Things

Our body is a mechanism full of wonders. It constantly sends us signals. If you are still bothered by your past or if there is something you haven't forgiven yourself for, your body may give you signs. You might have recognized these signs: headaches, nausea, trouble sleeping, and lack of appetite. These symptoms are warnings indicating that you need to work on your inner peace.

Physically pleasant things are a great way to combat symptoms of anxiety, stress, unforgiveness and many other self-sabotaging acts. Relaxation techniques that you enjoy doing will help you calm your thoughts and put your spirit at ease. For some of us, taking a long bubble bath is fine. Some of us love running and other types of exercise, all of which can be helpful for sleep problems. Meditation is also a great choice, along with walking, dancing or eating your favorite food. As I've said, anything that works for you is the perfect option.

Relaxing activities may seem insignificant when it comes to the issue of forgiving yourself, but scholar Alfred Korzybski once said, "God may forgive you your sins, but your nervous system won't." You can surely help your nervous system change its mind. Bring your body to a state of balance and calm to achieve inner peace. Another reason for pursuing peace & serenity is very simple and logical; you will feel good in your skin. If you are comfortable in your body, you have the fullest potential to feel comfortable about your mind as well. The past will be there; somewhere in the corner of your mind, but it won't be something that gives you troubles.

Step Seven: Communicate with Your Closest Friends

When we make a mistake and become self-accusatory, we may not see things clearly. Our mistake often seems a lot bigger than it is. Your friends or relatives can help you. They see your troubles from a different perspective; therefore, they cannot alter the way you see things. Some of them will bring you an abundance of positive energy that will comfort you. Some of them will give you advice to cope with your pain. Some of them will, perhaps, point out important elements of your mistakes. Each of these options is perfectly normal and welcome, even those friends who criticize you—if they are your true friends and want to help you—it can make a positive impact. Friends are there to understand you, even when you cannot understand yourself. Let them these friends work their magic. They can help you unleash your optimism.

These friends can be very valuable to you in increasing your possibility. In talking with them, they will be open minded and non-judgmental of the past experiences or behaviors that you might not be proud of. Enjoy being with good people and let your strict criteria loose. If they accept you in spite of your past transgressions, you should also be compassionate and forgiving toward yourself. You are not alone in your troubles. Feel free to use all the help you can get – people who appreciate and love you will be there to bring out the best in you.

Step Eight: Self-Forgiveness Is a Part of Your Higher Purpose

If you don't find any reason justifiable enough to forgive yourself, consider the fact that our Creator has a higher purpose for all of us, and fulfilling that greater purpose depends on our willingness to accept our life's path. Our path will have numerous obstacles. You had something difficult in your past, but you being here today clearly show it's not the end. You will experience many hurdles and numerous tests. Your future obstacles may be challenging enough; don't meet them with your past burden. Your past is just a hurdle to overcome and an opportunity to prepare you for your next hurdle. Conquer it once and for all, and this will help prepare you for the future.

If you want to fulfill your highest purpose and get into the depths of your being as you are reaching the peak of your potential, you must not look back. The sooner you decide to get rid of the heavyweights of your past days, the higher you will FLY. When nothing works in your favor, feel what your spirit is telling you. Your spirit wants to be free. It wants to take you down the road of self-love and up the mountain of self-appreciation. You deserve to let the essence of your being to be happy.

You have all the love and support of your Creator. Your destiny is written in time, and if you know how to accept it, you will go far. If you learn how to be independent of your past, you will go even farther.

F.L.Y. Challenge Testimonial: Donna Fox-Scott, Alabama

I would like to introduce you to a wonderful lady named Donna Fox-Scott, who was kind enough to share her experience with the Journey to Self-Love Challenge with all of us. Her testimonial is another confirmation that this challenge was mutual satisfaction for all of us who participated.

Why Donna? Because of her story, like every woman's story is unique and deserves to be told. Her experience is one to which many can relate. It does not mean her life is average and her problems too common—quite the opposite, because she managed to overcome many common setbacks and obstacles. Donna decided to face the challenges. She was determined to get to a higher level of self- love, and she was very honest with herself. It wasn't blindly following my challenge program; she was really engaged with it. Her effort, sincere devotion, and freeing results makes her story special. I appreciate her kindness to share her experience with us, especially because it can be a direct illustration of this chapter and all the sentiments about letting the past go.

You see, the past is not only about the problems we had. It is also about every part of our lifestyle we were not happy with. Maybe we were shy, maybe we were overwhelmed by other people's influence, or maybe we were passive. With deliberate effort, we can put all those factors behind us just like Donna did.

Here is what she says about her self-discovery through the Journey to Self-Love Challenge:

> *The challenge for me was one of the most inspiring things I had done all year! I learned not to feel guilty about decisions and choices I've made in my life, and to honor myself and what I want in my future. I'd been the mother, nurturer, and the go-to person for everybody in my family. I had to look around and see who was standing on their own two feet or still depending on me. This challenge helped me decide and showed me how to let go without feeling guilty or wondering how I would be perceived by those I chose to let go of. I looked forward to our daily assignments and enjoyed going within to find the peace, love, and joy that I desire for my life!*

Love Notes to Self

_____

_____

_____

_____

_____

_____

_____

_____

_____

_____

_____

_____

_____

_____

Love Notes to Self

_____

_____

_____

_____

_____

_____

_____

_____

_____

_____

_____

_____

_____

_____

_____

_____

_____

_____

Chapter Five
Protecting Your Treasures

My Dearest Sister:

There are some things that must never be compromised; jewels that the Creator has placed inside of you. Your values, self-respect, self-love and dignity are the most sacred parts of who you are. It's time to rediscover those precious pearls. Cleanse your spirit and repair the damage that has been caused by traumatic relationships, betrayals, poor choices, and low self-image.

The season for healing is now. Purge your spirit. Turn everything off and sit alone with your thoughts. The poet Rumi said "Silence is the language of God, anything else is just a poor translation." You do not need to talk about your pain another day. Simply make time for yourself to dwell in peace and quiet. Acknowledge your emotions and accept how you feel. Acceptance is the first step in any therapeutic process. There is healing in solitude and there is restoration in stillness. Silence the chaos and create a clear channel so the Spirit can speak to you.

With the information overload culture we live in today, it's easy for negative images and events to impede on our subconscious mind. Remember your mind is fragile. It is imperative that you guard it from distractions, negativity, and foolishness. Tense and stress- filled thoughts are the primary cause of dis-ease in the body. Being selective about what you allow to enter your mind is an important part of the self-love process. To maintain a balanced mental state, you must stay focused on what's important and refuse to allow the distractions of television, gossip, and time wasting to take up residence in our mind. An alternative to watching TV and nonproductive Internet surfing is to write down your thoughts, ideas, and feelings. When you express yourself in writing, you are putting your mind at ease. Or perhaps take a peaceful walk by yourself. Your mind is most relaxed when you are alone. Solitude seems to be a lost art, but some of the most profound things occur within you when you are alone.

Solitude:

- Gives you an outlet to find peace and mental relaxation.

- Allows you to know yourself and connect more intimately.

- Encourages reflection on past experiences challenging you to face your vulnerabilities.

- Enhances time to connect with your mind, body, and spirit without sensory distractions.

- Stimulates the greatest part of your creativity.

- Separates you from others and helps you tap into your own truth without being influenced.

You can welcome solitude first by shutting off all communication with other people. Challenge yourself to do this at least once per week. Some examples of outlets to disconnect are social media, cell phones, computers, and any other outlets where you could be contacted.

Meditation

Incorporating meditation as a daily ritual can help you get into a relaxing state and sync your spiritual, mental and physical energy. The world is very fast-paced, and the pressure of trying to maintain all of the responsibilities and roles you have can cause added stress.

Rhythmic breathing with your eyes closed as you meditate creates a bridge to inner peace. Maintaining this peace can be a difficult task in the midst of upholding all the expectations life requires of you.

Meditation can also help build the mental and spiritual resilience to keep you rejuvenated and ready to interact with the world. You can begin meditating either in a group or on your own. It doesn't require a lot of time to meditate and get the most out of it. It might be difficult for you to focus and sit still initially, but as you continue to meditate, it will become more natural. Try it for maybe five minutes, and then as the days go on increase it by intervals of five minutes. Work your way up to 15-20 minutes. As you become more connected to your inner self and spirit, self-love will naturally flourish.

Elevating Your Thoughts

Have you ever wanted to do something, but then talked yourself out of it?

I'm too busy. No one will listen to me. I don't have the training.

Can you admit that your thinking has been small and limited? Has mediocrity attacked your behaviors? Perhaps you have allowed low-level thinking to poison your mind. Do even the smallest challenges cause you to feel defeated? If your answer is YES, then it's time you make some drastic changes. You have the power to transform your life by elevating your thoughts and speaking words of power to yourself. As you recognize the need to take your thoughts and language higher, you will begin to self-correct and positively impact your confidence and behavior.

One of my favorite quotes by Ramez Sasson says, *"Your mind is your instrument; learn to be its master, not its slave."*

Taking control over your mind and thoughts means using discipline and focus to reject less than pleasant images and thoughts from taking root in your mind. No negative thought can dwell without your permission, therefore, once you make a commitment to monitor your thoughts, you will be able to take your life to the next level. If self-discipline challenges you, remind yourself that if you brush your teeth on a regular basis, you are disciplined. The next step is choosing to be disciplined in other areas.

Take a moment and think about your goals and dreams. What do you want to accomplish in the next few weeks, months, or years? Can you expand your thoughts and use your imagination to your advantage by visualizing yourself accomplishing all the things you've ever dreamed? If you're working on completing an academic degree, visualize yourself walking across the stage receiving it. The more real you make the experience, the more excitement you will feel, and the thrill of obtaining the goal in your mind will motivate you to do whatever is required to achieve the goal you have visualized for your life.

There is something magnificent about elevating your thoughts. It can cause you to think bigger and believe in yourself. Always remember that you have unique, valuable, and remarkable gifts and talents that need your attention. Once you retrain your thinking, you will realize some things about yourself you don't even know right now. There are people in the world who are doing far more than you are with fewer resources, skills, and talents. Don't sell yourself short. Get excited about the possibilities of a larger more fulfilled life. If you know your worth, go out and get it. Increase your belief in yourself.

Clean Out and Get Organized

When you get rid of old things, you make room for new things. By cleaning out what you don't need, the Law of Attraction is activated, and you create an opportunity to add more value to your life. The Law of Attraction is the ability to attract into our lives whatever we are focusing on. Cleaning and organizing your home, office, car, and other personal spaces can give you a feeling of dominion and increase your attraction to what you truly desire. It helps you feel in control of your life and surroundings. Cleaning and organizing can set the stage for you to become more assertive, neat, and confident in all areas of life. When you hold onto things you don't need, you are subconsciously reinforcing a mindset of lack that keeps you mentally stagnant.

About three years ago, I came to the realization that I am what I like to call a premature hoarder. To this day, I make a conscious effort to throw away my children's school papers, give away the clothes they've outgrown, and pass their gently used toys along. It's something I struggle with. Not just with my children's belongings but also my own. I make a deliberate effort to be disciplined and follow through with cleaning out old items. I actually have myself on a schedule. Every six months, I go through our house and pack up clothes that have been outgrown, recycle the children's unwanted paper, and create space for new energy and a renewed sense of organization and structure.

Entrusting Your Body to Others

Sometimes circumstances and life events can cause us to be vulnerable with the wrong people for the wrong reasons. That's why it's necessary that you have a principle-based set of guidelines to help protect you from people who might attempt to misuse you. Be selective about who you allow to enter your personal space. Be mindful that just because a man desires you, that doesn't necessarily mean he values you. As a verb, the definition of desire is to "strongly wish for or to want," and synonyms are coveted, yearn, want, and so on. To be desired is a wonderful thing, and there is nothing wrong with wanting to be yearned for or desired. But in this context, the verbal use of value means, "Consider (someone or something) to be important or beneficial; have a high opinion of," with alternative verbs being appreciated, esteem, and respect. Value comes in three phases: appraisal, assessment, and investment. Essentially, if a man hasn't taken the time to get know you, connect with your uniqueness, and then invest in you from a genuine space within him, he's more than likely not someone you want to risk being vulnerable with.

I'd like to share a personal story with you from my youth. At one point in my life, it was difficult for me to discuss this because I felt ashamed. Just the thought of the experience brought on feelings of disgust. As I mentioned earlier, when I was in my late teens, before I incorporated personal development as a part of my lifestyle, I had no idea what it meant to know my worth, value my uniqueness, or celebrate who I was. I misused my body by having sex with men who I knew did not value me. Somewhere in my mind, I thought it would give me fulfillment. Doesn't this sound like a story you could hear in almost every college dorm? We know this should not be the case, and at some point as women, we must set higher standards.

Setting higher standards starts with being patient and discerning before you do or say something without considering the consequences. For example, be careful saying I love you prematurely when dating, no matter how handsome or funny the guy is. He might seem like the man of your dreams, but you don't know him well enough to be sure. You also should be selective about giving the gift of sensual, physical love before you know to whom you are giving it. Intimacy is a beautiful thing when you are sharing it with someone who knows how to appreciate such moments with you. To be sure, you must know how to approach your partner. Being careful is the key. No matter how much you desire to be with someone, if you don't want to get hurt, you need to know if the person feels the same. What can you do? You can separate true attention from crafty flirting, real appreciation from casual relationships, and physical attraction from true passion and desire. Forget about romantic movies and pink sunglasses. These things only perpetuate a false sense of reality. Reconcile your heart's desires with the messages of your wisdom and rationality.

It is up to you to set the standard for how other people treat you. When you value your body and use discernment regarding who you allow to share your temple, you are honoring yourself in a way that only you can do from a place of confidence and positive self-image. Show others that you know your worth. Protect your body; it is the temple of your spirit. It's the only shell you will have as long as you're alive. It is the first representation of yourself the world sees. Treat your body well. Take pride in caring for your skin and hair. Use oils that bring out the natural beauty in your skin. Keep your hair strong strong and healthy. Cherish your devotion to your inner beauty and think twice before you decide to let a random man into your sacred space.

Modern lifestyle implies that meaningless sex is the most common way of having fun. As we mature, we might learn some painful truths about that fact. First of all, it is never just fun. It is sharing your most valuable treasures with someone who cannot cherish you at the level you should be cherished. It can leave emotional scars for life. Feeling used and rejected are common consequences of menial relationships. Even if you felt like it was a cool thing at that moment, you might feel it wasn't such a good choice as you continue to evolve. At least I did, and I am so thankful, but it wasn't always that way.

I went on for many years, looking for things in other people that could only come from within. It wasn't until I was in my early 30's that I began to cultivate myself through personal development, meditation, and elevated self-awareness. I discovered the truth of who I am, and I realized the value I possess must be realized and expressed by me first before I could look for anyone else to appreciate it.

Here's some good news, you don't have to get into emotional frailties like I did. If you are struggling with similar problems, I hope this book will help you become stronger than you are right now. My desire is for you to be more independent and brave enough to protect your body from meaningless interactions, and guard your spirit against being damaged. Remember, going from bed to bed cannot fill the void that true self-love will. You can obtain short-term pleasure, but you deserve so much better.

Know Your Worth

The more deeply you value yourself, the more other people will value you. Take into account all your skills, talents, and gifts. Each of us has something special, God-given. Treasure such traits and use them. Some of us are good listeners, while some of us cook great meals but everything counts. If you are good at something and you enjoy doing it, this is a testament of how your natural gifts can bring you joy and happiness.

Believe in yourself and constantly treat yourself as though you are worthy of the very best. Maintain a healthy optimistic attitude as much as possible. Speak life and abundance when you speak to yourself and others. Don't sell yourself short because other people can't appreciate what you have to offer. The people who do this are usually those who haven't discovered their own talents and purpose, so they feel the need to belittle others as a way to feel good about themselves. Don't judge them and don't hate them. Love yourself instead. Maybe they will find inspiration in you. After all, self-respect can be influential. When other people see that you treat yourself well and that you make it a requirement for others to do the same, it could inspire them to do the same.

Your conversations are a good place to start. When you're discussing your worth, be firm and reassured. Make sure you are always confident about the value you bring. Be mindful not to allow others to misuse you or take what you have to offer for granted. As you begin to reinforce your standards to others, you'll notice your level of self-love will soar. Your self-esteem will be heightened, and you'll feel empowered and more confident. Nothing says I love me like confidence and knowledge of self-worth. Spend time working on yourself. Read things that motivate and encourages you. Watch good movies and listen to music that moves you. Establish new rituals when you wake up in the morning. The way you start your day is important; it lays the foundation for the whole day. Take time to listen to motivational messages that uplift you and get you to the place where you can see a larger vision of yourself.

I wake up every morning at 6:00 a.m. I meditate for 15

minutes, listen to a motivational message for another 15 minutes, and then I exercise for 30 minutes. These disciplines help shape my day. Meditation puts my mind and spirit at ease. The motivational videos provide inspiration, and they empower and enable me to face the day. When I exercise, I feel challenged because I really don't enjoy it. Therefore, when I do exercise I feel like I've accomplished something meaningful, and this helps establish momentum for the rest of the day.

You can do something equally as empowering. Find your own rituals and schedule them as you wish. Maybe you prefer to listen to motivational messages in the evening, right before you go to bed. Maybe this helps you to have sweet dreams and wake up fresh and full of energy.

Such rituals and practices are a huge part of building confidence in your own worth. If you can stay consistent, you can prove to yourself that you are strong, persistent, and devoted. With all those honorable traits, you can cause an overall positive shift to occur.

Let Faith Be Your Guide

Your ability to believe in those things you can't see is a treasure and an essential element in the process of self-love. It is beyond imagination. It is like having a unique sense. Faith and the ability to believe in yourself and your abilities are going to be a huge part of your self-love journey. During this journey, you can write a new chapter of your life. Be determined to breathe life into your dream(s), and set your life in a new direction. Inside of you is a sense that your ideas are valuable, and the goals you have for your life are possible. Perhaps you've allowed fear to suffocate your faith, and complacency has undermined your commitment to achieving your goal.

Take a look at all the possibilities. It's still possible to start or establish your business. It's still possible to heal and sustain your marriage or to kick the addiction that has entrapped you. With faith in your heart and a made up mind, impossible is a foreign word, which cannot be translated to the language of your soul. It speaks words like success, ambition, and motivation. Let your soul speak. You will hear wonderful and inspirational thoughts—

great guidelines for your dreams.

All you need to do is summon the faith to believe. It doesn't have to be a lot of faith, just the size of a mustard seed. Once you have a small amount of faith, embrace the disciplines and behaviors that are necessary to bring forth results. Read the books, take the classes, and seek out the professionals that can help you manifest your vision. Faith is a tool you can use to make things happen. It is a free tool that costs you giving up pessimism. That's a bargain. Just the fact that you have a strong belief can force the Universe to yield and manifest what you believe. I've seen it happen in my life many times.

Here is an example:

This year, my family and I celebrated five years that we've been living in our home. I remember like it was yesterday when we lived in a two-bedroom apartment that had become cluttered. I began to feel like the walls were closing in on us. It was a claustrophobic feeling. It was a small space that became uncomfortable to maneuver around on a daily basis. Our children barely had anywhere to play outside or just to run around and have fun as kids.

I remember joking with my husband saying, *"If either of us brings anything else in this apartment, even another pencil, I think I'm going to lose my mind."*

That was when we decided that we needed to make a change. The year was 2010, and President Obama established the New Home Buyers Tax Credit. The guideline was as long as we closed on our house before July 1, we would be eligible to receive the $8,000 tax credit. We looked around at different homes for almost five months, but practically every house we looked at was old, or it just wasn't a place we could call "home."

At one point we began to get discouraged because the credit score requirement was 620, but no matter how much debt I paid off, I couldn't seem to get my score above 616. But we refused to give up on the idea of a better life for our family. It was time to fix things and find our peace were in. At the beginning of June, and

July 1st was quickly drawing closer. Although we were facing a below-par credit score and we couldn't seem to find a house, we kept looking and believing for a favorable outcome.

One day I was talking to my godmother, and she asked what was going on with the house. I told her about the situation with my credit score, and she said, "That'll be easy to fix, I'll just add you to my credit card, and it'll look like you've been a cardholder for the last two years that I've had the card. That should bring your score up at least five or six points.

She added me to her card, and within a few weeks, my credit score was up to 622. That eliminated the credit score obstacle, but by this point, we were in mid-June, and we still hadn't put a bid on a house. We were getting a little nervous, but still, our faith was relentless. We found our house on June 17th, and we closed on June 30th. One more day, and we would have been ineligible for the tax credit. When I think about how this happened, I know there was supernatural intervention working on our behalf. The timing of it all was simply remarkable. It was our firm belief that manifested our desire. We had been through days when we could not sleep well, and being overwhelmed by fear that we wouldn't be able to make the deadline. We also had many days and nights dreaming of our better life, in vivid colors—almost like we were already there. The faith remained. We knew we had worked hard for it and we believed it would happen.

It's possible to exercise faith and manifest things in your life, not just material things but intangibles as well. If you believe for healing, peace of mind, or the spirit to forgive, your faith alone will activate the magnetism that can draw you closer to your desire.

Find Your Life's Purpose

It's critical for you to get connected with your life's purpose so that you can create the ideal life for yourself and operate from a place of fulfillment and meaning purpose. There is a reason you were born. You are destined to fulfill a purpose, and it is your responsibility to get connected with this purpose and create a sense of direction and meaning in your life. When you look back on your life five years from now, you should have a favorable response when you ask, *"If I were no longer here, would people remember me for making the world better in some way?"* At some point, you will reflect on your life and say, "What am I doing in my life that will be impactful to others?"

You'll want to get clarity on your life, what you should be doing at this stage you're currently in, and you'll want to hold yourself accountable while walking the road to your destiny. You don't want to realize that you have settled into a career that you consider boring and unfulfilling. Most people stay on jobs for years doing work they hate, either because they don't know what their life's purpose is, or they are too fearful to step out and live from their heart and not their mind. Our mind can sometimes lead us down a path that is displeasing to our heart. Many people settle for less in life and deprive the world of their gifts, talents, and creativity. It's unfortunate. No one knows what great impact they could have had once the time and opportunity had passed.

Let's face it, we cannot all invent Cancer drugs or new machines, but we can all make a contribution, and even the smallest contribution matters because in truth, there's nothing small about sowing into others with your gift. Discovering your purpose should go hand-in-hand with utilizing and maximizing your talents. If you have the talent to bring laughter and joy to people through entertainment, you should pursue this wholeheartedly. Every gift we have is meant to make the world better in some way. The way to know if you are operating in your purpose is if what you're doing focuses more on serving and empowering other people than being just about earning money or how it makes you feel.

In this chapter, you'll see me refer to my life's purpose as my work. The late Dr. Myles Munroe said, *"Your job is what they pay you to do, your work is what you were born to do. Find your work and make it your job, and you'll never worry about getting fired. You can get fired from your job, but you can never get fired from your gift."*

It's not always easy to find your life's purpose, and when you do, it will be a process of transitioning it into your work. That's okay because this is required for you to walk in your destiny and fulfill your greatest purpose. When you decide you're tired of living life aimlessly and take action to get connected with your purpose, you are making the statement: I love me!

Several years ago I worked for a well-known telecommunications company. They paid very well, and the benefits were excellent. My job required that I work on the phone in a cubicle all day answering calls from belligerent customers, who I was required to sell to before I ended the call. After the first 6–12 months of working there, I was burned out. Because of low seniority, I was required to work a lot of overtime, and the shift I was assigned was not conducive to living a well-balanced lifestyle. About two and a half years into my employment, the company offered a severance package. I was one of the first employees to sign up because I knew my life had a greater purpose than sitting in front of a computer all day listening to irate customers call me insulting names. Maybe some people would be content defusing irate customer complaints, but for me, it was a tiring experience.

At that point in my life, I still didn't know what my life's purpose was, but I knew for sure that the job I was doing, was not it because it would never be rewarding. I appreciated the opportunity to make a living, but I didn't identify with the job in any way. Most of my family family and friends could not understand why I decided to walk away from this job which most of them considered to be "good." They said I was being foolish, and I was, in terms of this society obsessed with job security. But, in reality, considering what I was striving for, I made a good choice. I've never regretted leaving that job, and I realize it was part of the process for me to find my real purpose. I've learned that it really is not my concern or duty to convince other people to understand my choices. My responsibility is to honor my right to live a purpose-driven life on my own terms.

When you discover your passion and decide to pursue it, be mindful that some people in your life might not be excited for you or supportive of your vision and the things you want to accomplish. As your vision gets wider, your circle will get smaller. Your ambition and success will cause you to lose some people, and others will belittle your accomplishments in an attempt to destroy your confidence. Don't let this discourage or upset you. In fact, let it reassure you that you're on the right path. When you hear non-constructive criticism, have compassion for the person speaking to you, as they are merely expressing their own personal feelings of inadequacy.

Remember, while you have been able to travel the journey of self-love, many other people are still suffering with low self-worth and possibility blindness. They can't see themselves past their comfort zone, and they might feel intimidated by the thought of your success.

Never become overly dependent on praise or criticism; relying on either of them too much is a sign of weakness. Keep your vision clear and know your steps are being ordered. You have an assignment, and it was given to you to fulfill. Sometimes you might be the only one who sees or believes in it, but that's okay because there's a planned Divine purpose for your life. Stay focused and keep moving forward.

Exercise, Eat Well, Treat Your Body Like the Temple It Is

I'm sure you know firsthand that stress can have a negative impact on your body. Worry about paying bills, or the drama of strained relationships over the course of time will begin to show on your face through age lines and dark circles under your eyes. Depriving yourself of adequate rest and sleep will lead your body to tell the story of your neglect. Smoking, abusing alcohol and drugs, and poor eating will all wear on your body after a while. Discipline yourself to make healthy choices that promote wellness and keep you looking youthful and radiant no matter what's happening in your life. This discipline should be a lifestyle so that it doesn't get put on the back burner when you're going through extra stressful times.

We all have our weaknesses for certain things that aren't good for us, but the key is to be disciplined. I'm not recommending that you use drugs in moderation by any means. Food and other less harmful elements can be enjoyed in moderation without adverse effects. Eat as you love yourself.

Take in foods that are rich in nutrition, antioxidants, fiber, and necessary vitamins. It is natural to feel the urge to indulge in some not-so-healthy treats now and then. Enjoying the not-so-healthy treats when you're in a state of calm is less harmful to you emotionally and physically than indulging when you're stressed. Nonetheless, you must make a commitment not only to eat healthy most of the time but to adopt a healthy lifestyle.

You might have noticed that when you exercise, you feel more energetic and exuberant. That's because your body releases chemicals called endorphins when you're working out. Endorphins evoke positive feelings in the brain that are very similar to the effects of morphine. This is one of many reasons you should stay active. Start with a realistic goal you know you will stick to, and test yourself. For example, if your goal is to incorporate more exercise into your life, you might want to start with 15-20 minutes of physical activity at least three days per week.

Decide which days you want to workout, and put yourself on a time frame to measure your commitment level. If you keep a calendar for other life appointments, make an appointment with yourself that cannot be interfered with as if you're meeting your boss (because you are, You!) Consider starting with 15 or 30 days. The more you keep your body active, the better you will feel about yourself and your ability to stay committed to improving the way your body feels. I like to refer to this as "healthy momentum."

A healthy spirit must live in a healthy body. When you harm your body, even unintentionally, your spirit loses its calm. When you eat improper food, your thoughts are bothered by unpleasant aches and nausea. When you are too lazy, your mind could get lazy, too. But when you keep your body strong and vibrant you will think clearly and focus better. Unfortunately, many people don't realize this until the challenge appears so great that they don't even try or worse, it is too late, and they are no longer with us. Hopefully, one day you will be able to help them as well, for now, you can help them indirectly by ensuring you are treating your body properly, like a temple.

When it comes to exercise, your options are limitless. You don't have to be a professional athlete, run a marathon, and lift weights. A word of caution, while researching exercises that may help you obtain your health goals, avoid starting with extra-difficult cardio training or exercises you aren't physically ready for. Not being able to fulfill these challenging physical activities will counter your goal and put you at risk emotionally and physically. You know the cycle, the feeling of discouragement when a goal cannot be achieved, and potentially giving up. It is more manageable to go step-by-step. Thinking things through and formulating a realistic and practical regimen is always the first step. If you need help with formulating a plan or being accountable, research a trainer.

Think about your current physical activity. How fit are you? Could you run for half an hour without stopping? If you haven't been active lately, you should definitely start by doing easier exercise programs. There's no shame in that. You have to start to get where you want to go. Yoga is a great starting point. If you decide yoga is suitable for you, you still have to decide what kind of yoga will work best for you. Do you want stretching or would you prefer to test the limits of your strength? You choose. Even if you hate sports and exercise, the importance of physical activities still applies to you. Simple walking or gardening counts as well as other physical activities like playing with your children or walking up and down stairs at work. As I've mentioned earlier in this chapter regular 15-minute intervals of exercise is a great and effective start. The important piece is to keep your body occupied, active and consistent.

You are probably already aware of the importance of a proper diet. The word diet usually sounds very rigorous and tasteless, but it doesn't have to be. First of all, media has distorted what you think about when you hear the word diet. I simply means what you're eating every day; it does not have to mean deprivation and restriction. The Creator has provided us with food from the earth, but we added impurities. Getting back to nature's food could be a worthwhile improvement to your life.

If I ask," Will you give up sugar?"

Your answer could be, "I'll think about it."

What if I ask, "Would you give up health risks?"

Of course you would.

You don't have to give up sugar, or anything else, but you should eat in moderation. Personally, I don't believe implementing a healthy diet is as difficult as we make it. It's not necessary to stick to a rigorous diet plan to stay healthy. You should first educate yourself about the basic principles of healthy eating. Since we live in the Internet era, it's easier than ever to research and learn about anything. You can find out everything about fruits, vegetables, vitamins, minerals, as well as all the other do's and don't's of the food pyramid in very affordable or free e-books, articles, or from your physicians. Most importantly, listen to your body, it sends you clear signals when you eat something it doesn't like. The key is to make a conscious decision to eat healthier. Implement your decision step-by-step and don't stop until you know your diet is good for you.

Finally, cherish your body. Love everything about it, even imperfections. Embrace that the Creator gave it to us in order to makes us unique. Forget perfect women from magazines. They live in photographs only. Outside those pages, they might be even more insecure than the average woman—imagine you looked perfect on those photos, but you seemed like a different person live. That might come across to others that you are not genuine.

We cannot escape from all those perfect bodies. They are everywhere—TV, commercials, the Internet, movies, and magazines, but in most cases, those bodies are not real. We often forget those perfect bodies are products of well-developed photo and video editing software. The Creator has given us various shapes of beauty. Beautiful means unique and it doesn't have anything to do with your weight, tan, hair color, the shape of your body, the size of your nose, or any other physical traits. Each of those traits can be beautiful—and are—if you accept them and are proud of them. A chubby girl can look great in the same dress a model wears, only if she feels comfortable wearing it. It is not about how you look, but how you feel. Acceptance is the key because it leads to greater confidence. More than likely, people don't notice your flaws if you don't point them out. Charisma, energy, and being authentic are more important than physical appearance. As you learn to accept yourself, you don't exercise to look like a supermodel, but to feel healthy and be at your best.

FLY women don't have a reason to feel bad in their skin. We embrace every inch of who we are. Go ahead, indulge your body; give it the best treatments and sensations. Take long bubble baths and use perfumes that enhance your gracefulness. Walk or run and dance if you wish. Feed your body the best nutrients and natural foods from the earth. Drink enough water. Listen to your body's whispers. Your mind, body, and spirit deserve all the goodness you can afford.

Because You Are Worth It

Buy yourself flowers. Why wait for a romantic partner to buy you flowers? Buy yourself flowers as an "I love me" gift. Have them in your living space to brighten up the rooms and add a touch of nature's beauty. Set a bouquet of flowers on your desk at work. Get closer with nature, and enjoy the beauty of a simple, affordable bouquet. If you decide to buy them for yourself, it's a great confirmation of self-love, and you'll admit, is pretty refreshing.

Flowers have the natural beauty and fragrance that can help you feel better and freshen the air. As you do more loving things for yourself, your love for yourself will strengthen, and it will become more natural for you to express how you feel about yourself and embrace your self-worth. Here is a list of flowers and colors of flowers and what they represent:

Heather Lavender symbolizes admiration, solitude, and beauty while white heather symbolizes protection and indicates that wishes will come true.

Iris symbolizes eloquence. Purple iris is symbolic of wisdom and compliments. Blue iris symbolizes faith and hope.

Yellow iris symbolizes passion while white iris symbolizes

purity.

Carnation symbolizes pride and beauty. A red carnation symbolizes love, pride, and admiration, and a pink carnation symbolizes the love of a woman or a mother.

Bouvardia double symbolizes enthusiasm. It is also used to indicate zest for life.

Aster symbolizes patience. It is indicative of a love of variety. It also symbolizes elegance and daintiness.

Amaryllis is symbolic of splendid beauty. It is also used to indicate worth beyond beauty.

Use the list of flowers and their meanings to send yourself the flowers that best symbolize how you feel about yourself or to remind you of an area in your life that you are currently developing. What a beautiful and clever reminder.

Quality Time With That Special Someone

Add yourself to your priority list. Schedule a "me day." You cannot possibly have time for yourself if you are always catering to the needs of others. To keep yourself fresh, rejuvenated, and fulfilled, you must make it a priority to set aside personal time for yourself. Sometimes you should redirect your focus single-mindedly on your own spiritual, mental and physical well-being. Take time every evening to create a space of peace around your home through prayer, meditation, or just sitting in solitude. Turn the television, computer, and radio off for the evening. There are certain calls you don't need to answer. Allow your evenings to be peaceful, and use this time to build the mental and spiritual resiliency that will serve as your strength for the next day.

Make some time during the day to be free of other people. Do whatever you want; analyze what is happening during your day or simply relax. If you can take 15 minutes or half an hour to spend with yourself, this will increase your peace of mind. It can help you put up with the daily routine and refresh your mind. Simply take a short break during the day, and enjoy the privilege of being alone. Pressing the pause button for such a short time can be really useful, but you should think bigger and devote whole mobile-free, people-free, care- free days to yourself.

When you set aside time to do something just for you, this is a lovely act of self-love. It's like taking yourself on a date for the entire day. Nobody can complement, entertain, and love you as you can. Take a whole day to yourself only doing things you enjoy. Look at your calendar and choose a day that works best. Choose carefully because it should be a day without any interruptions. It can be more fun to take time off work for your "me day" instead of scheduling it on the weekend. It's a subtle way of telling your boss: Today is all about me. Be sure to schedule it well in advance so you have time to think about what you would like to do. Write down your plans, and have your day organized so you can maximize the time. Get excited and anticipate spending the day with yourself and doing those things that make you happy. On this day, you will not run any errands or do any chores. Your main concern is to enjoy your day to the fullest.

Many people find it difficult to accept their right to "me day." The whole point of achieving self-love is accepting you deserve the best. "Me day" is a great way to elevate the level of self-love, get to know your needs and desires better, and enjoy your life. Another way to show yourself love is by writing yourself a love letter. Love letters are easy ways to deliver messages with heartfelt meaning. Write yourself short love notes in the form of a traditional letter or affirmation form. Nope, not an email! Paper lasts, and it is tangible proof of affirmation and heartfelt feelings about you. Highlight all the things you are proud of yourself for; you might also want to include areas you want to master. Here is an example:

Dear Self (or even write your name here):

You are so beautiful and kind. I enjoy spending time with you. I appreciate your authenticity and your efforts to be the best that you can be. Your spirit is so compassionate, and you are always positive and reassured. Your energy is contagious and you attract success and abundance. You have something special that the world is waiting for you to bring forth. You are unique and fabulous. You are like no other, and I will always take care of you. I love you.

Sounds silly, but nobody said self-love and self-appreciation should not be interesting, and even silly at least a little bit. Writing love notes to yourself is fun, and it's a sure way to bring a smile to your face.

It might feel uncomfortable at first, just like many of the other self-love rituals. That's because you've never been taught how to love and appreciate yourself from the inside out genuinely. We've been taught love from the outside and hope the inside is just as nice. This experience is similar to starting a new romance and all the ways you would show that love interest how you felt about them. That's the same way you have to express love to yourself. The more you do it the more natural it will become.

Journey to Self-Love Challenge Testimonial

Michelle Blount's words regarding the self-love challenge are very profound. She had a life altering experience:

> *The Journey to Self-Love Challenge was such a challenging and intense exercise for me, as I peeled back years and layers of tunnel vision based upon ideals, Folkways, rules and Mores. I picked up limiting beliefs throughout my life from my sisters, aunties, neighbors, faculty, church members, co-workers- mommy, granny, and everyone in-between. My thoughts and prayers expressed my longing for an awakening and an honest conversation with myself. As a result of the challenge, I was able to confront vulnerable parts of myself, acknowledge and embrace my authenticity and get reconnected with the woman I would like to be.*

Love Notes to Self

Love Notes to Self

_____

_____

_____

_____

_____

_____

_____

_____

_____

_____

_____

_____

_____

_____

_____

_____

Chapter Six
The F.L.Y. Lifestyle

My Dearest Sister:

Today is the day to start over! Recommit to your commitments! You can't keep pretending you're happy with the way things are going right now. It shows on your face, in your walk, conversation, and everything you do. If this goes on too long, it will turn into resentment and you don't want to live with resentment and bitterness for the rest of your life.

Start new today! Get your priorities back in order and recharge your momentum and ambition! Speak life over your dreams, goals, and your destiny.

Today seemingly simple tips and advice on how we should live can overwhelm us. Some of them are good, but many of these pointers lack insight. Why should we obey random rules, implement certain rituals, or practice some of those tips? Unfortunately, many people will conform, without any thought why these things matter. Sadly people expect instant happiness because they change certain habits according to some advice they've read online, in a book, or magazine. Where is true personal development in this simple scheme? Where is the glorious journey to self-love? It all sounds good in theory, but things are much more complex when practiced. If there is no real emotion, ambition, and deep desire to improve your life, it will be difficult to discover a sense of meaning.

Our lives consist of many factors, which govern our mental, physical, and emotional state – such as our eating and sleeping habits, preferences related to physical activities, our social life, and taste in various things, our attitudes, and moral standards. The abundance of such factors makes space for the uniqueness of our lifestyles. Unfortunately, balance in these areas is not vastly promoted. When we succumb to a low-level lifestyle, we are not grounded in terms of physical, mental and spiritual health. It causes huge cracks in our lives.

I believe the root cause of this problem lies in mechanical thinking and being seduced by empty promises from advice columns and tips. People don't realize they have to adjust tips they hear to their own preferences and needs. You wouldn't choose your doctor by his looks and seductive words, but by his ability to treat people, right, hopefully. Likewise, you shouldn't allow your emotions to choose your lifestyle elements by external factors, but by their ability to match your essence.

Imagine a world where everyone believed in themselves and their abilities without hesitation. Often, the lack of belief in oneself is perpetuated by the person's resistance to pointing areas that cause the feelings of depleted confidence. Most people are afraid to make key changes and accept the notion that true happiness is achievable. FLY women have, among other things, a mission to make their lifestyle match the balance of their self-loved personality. Once you fulfill your wonderful journey, adjusting your lifestyle habits will be a fun and rewarding transition. No fear, hesitation, or excuses—just pure joy of having the power to choose to live better.

Think about your current lifestyle. Are you satisfied? Do you think you spend enough time on things that matter to you? Are you well-organized? Most importantly, does your lifestyle include enough activities contributing to your personal development, inner balance, achieving and maintaining self-love? Right now, you may have to ponder the answers. Ideally, however, one day you will be able to say yes without thinking. Even when you are sure about your answer, you could still add new rituals to keep your lifestyle interesting and well- balanced.

Self-love is an ongoing journey. It lasts for a lifetime. It has some important checkpoints, such as when you realize you can love yourself unconditionally. I think that's something to celebrate! Luckily, this is not the end; only the beginning. There is a utopia when you love yourself with authenticity and without apology. You are more open to new experiences, you enjoy alone time more than ever, and you have a greater appreciation for the past, present, and future. Did I just say having an appreciation for the past? Yep, even for the past. Your lifestyle will reflect your commitment and new confidence. It will match the endless wealth of your spirit and soul. If you have been devoted to your journey, have faith that your lifestyle is becoming richer than ever. Keep making it better and remain diligent and consistent.

Your Inner Voice

You cannot escape your thoughts or emotions, so guide them in a way that works for you. Yes, you guide them they don't guide you. We all have a little voice in our head that can sometimes be too judgmental, belittling, or simply exasperating. Actually, it is an integral part of your subconscious mind. You cannot and should not shut that voice down completely, instead, learn to manage it. It is a sincere voice of your thoughts, so the only solution is to challenge your thoughts to be more pleasant. For example, when a negative voice creeps up, don't suppress it, it's trying to protect you, but prove it wrong by reminding yourself of a similar situation you encountered and conquered. Eventually, that fearful, self-protecting voice will slowly go away, and you will start to trust yourself. Start training your mind to believe in your capabilities, strength, and mental fortitude.

Instead of inundating your mind with dark thoughts about all the possible negative outcomes, try to focus on the opposite. When your mind asks why, ask it why not, so that your subconscious mind will ensure your "why not" comes true. Make room for light energy and encouraging thoughts, which will fuel you daily. The best part is that those thoughts are free. The only investment is your good will to succeed. It is imperative that you direct your thoughts to the flow of beauty and peace.

That is not something you can do overnight; it depends on various aspects; the good thing is you don't depend on anyone else. Thinking purposefully and positively results from building your personality to be strong and independent. Feed your faith and optimism, and you have already won half the battle. By making your system of beliefs firm and keeping your mind fresh and cheerful, you can easily maintain control over your thoughts. You can make them as warm and pleasant as you like. If it seems difficult, try to discover what stops you from achieving such mastery. Are you too self- judgmental? Are you troubled by thoughts that you don't deserve something? Detecting this limited thinking is a great first step.

Avoid negative emotions. You don't have a reason to feel inferior. You are uniquely and wonderfully made. Find a reason to believe that you deserve to be happy and do whatever makes you feel good provided it doesn't make you feel bad later. There are many reasons to put this into practice, even if you don't feel this way, do it anyway. If you have worked hard to achieve something, you deserve to enjoy it. Eliminate every thought that opposes your peace of mind. As you devote more attention to positive self-talk and giving yourself credit, it will become your natural habit.

Once you start feeling confident and self-assured, there is still a chance you could trip over your inner voice if you find yourself in a more complicated and challenging situation that brings more questions and dilemmas than your regular everyday life does. However, this should not burden you. When you are not sure about something, just ask yourself the following questions: "Am I disciplined? Am I focused? Do I have faith?"

If your answers are yes, relax and stay optimistic; if you answer No, you still have some work to do until you feel you can say yes three times. When you are answering these three questions, do not think about other people. Your mind and personality are unique, and your perspective is what's most important here. People have different understandings of discipline. For example, for some, sticking to a strict diet is difficult for them, while for others can program their minds and do not deviate from their plan. You measure your discipline by your goals; if your goal was to walk for an hour and you did it, you have been successful. Allow yourself to enjoy what it feels like to achieve that goal. You can pull on that feeling during the more difficult walking days. The same goes with the other two questions. You are only partially measured by your success. And always remember, your best **is** enough.

Feeding your mind with positive thoughts will strengthen your faith in the possibility of success. That is why fortifying your belief system is crucial. It has a direct impact on your thoughts.

Daily Affirmations

Say a nice thought, cause a nice thought.

Daily affirmations can be very helpful for strengthening your faith and keeping it in alignment with the words you are affirming. Words are much more than a means of communication. Experiments have shown positive words cause the release of endorphins, just as chocolate does. Good reason to keep my words sweet.

Besides choosing words carefully when you talk to other people, you should also take time for yourself and devote kind words to yourself. Daily affirmations have a significant impact on us. People usually define daily affirmations as phrases you think or say about yourself every day. I think daily affirmations are much more than this. In the beginning, they are just simple words. You make them come to life when you repeat and believe in them. It makes them important, and they become your personal mantra, which makes you stronger. They bring you more self-confidence and make you think about yourself as a beautiful woman who deserves pure joy. They are definitely more than motivational words; they are your intimate way to express self-love.

There is no ideal time of day to repeat affirmations. Some of us feel comfortable starting the day saying affirmations, while some of us sleep better if those affirmations are said before going to sleep. The truth is, you can repeat them anytime you want. The place is also not important; you can repeat them in your bedroom, bathroom, backyard, at work, on the bus—wherever you feel the need. You can use your mirror, or close your eyes. If you are in public, you don't have to say affirmations out loud. In my opinion, a cozy room with guaranteed privacy and calm atmosphere is a splendid place for such a ritual, just don't let "the right moment" or "perfect place" stop you from this practice. If you can take advantage of solitude or if you're not concerned about what people think of you, I would recommend saying your affirmations out loud. You can truly feel the power and truth in every word you say.

You can come up with your own affirmation. Just make sure that you can feel it and deeply relate to it. Choose words wisely and believe in them. Perhaps you can create different affirmations for the morning, evening, and special occasions. Keep them simple, powerful, present tense and, of course, be persistent.

Here are some examples of affirmations you can also use:

I am a beautiful, sincere and optimistic woman.

I will have an interesting and beautiful day.

I am responsible for my time; therefore, I will use it well.

I am ready for new adventures, challenges and knowledge.

My inner beauty will create beauty around me.

I am ready to make new friendships.

I am very positive.

I deserve to love and be loved.

I accept my good and bad sides and I expect others to accept me for who I am.

I am grateful for all the beauty in my life.

I have strong faith in the beauty of the whole humanity.

I embrace my Creator and His plans for me.

I will do every step I can in order to fulfill my higher purpose.

I accept my destiny, but I will do everything to make my life better.

I have the power to encourage myself and other people.

I feel free to say what I think.

I am not afraid to avoid unpleasant experiences and people who are trying to bring me down.

I feel comfortable to speak up for myself.

I live in harmony with other people, Universe and

my Creator.

I embrace this day as a new opportunity to explore
the beauty of being alive.

My soul and mind are open for new experiences.
You are your number one.

Put your heart's and soul's needs first.

Devoting time and attention to your own needs is not selfish,
it is natural. Just like you have to eat or sleep, you have to satisfy
your mental and spiritual needs as well. It is not just an
expression of self- love, and self-caring, it is also a basic human
need. How's that for perspective? A basic human need just as
sleep and water are.

Now, it seems like there is nothing to stop you from putting
your needs and caring for yourself, however, reality is very
complex. You often don't take the opportunity to deal with your
own needs because of other people. Just think about it: how many
times have you chosen to push down your own needs in order to
help someone else? The truth is, you should always make
yourself feel comfortable before helping others. It is not about
creating a balance between satisfying your own and other
people's needs. You should feel free to express your needs and
point out the importance of fulfilling them. Ignoring your own
needs brings a lot of frustrations and stress. Think about it, how
can you be the best friend, mother, or wife if your soul is lacking?
I'm sure that you have already found this to be difficult.

It's time to be assertive. Set the limit and let others know
when you are available to help them but don't hesitate to express
that you need some self-time. It is time to make your needs noted
and fulfilled. It will encourage others to be more considerate of
your needs as well. Embrace your right to stand up for your
needs, no matter how insignificant they seem. Believe me; if you
care about them, they are important because even the smallest of
your personal needs matter. It all works together to create a state
of personal satisfaction. If you ignore and neglect them, your
inner peace can be endangered, and your self-confidence will be

shaken. The more compromises you make, the faster it becomes your habit of putting yourself last. This habit is as destructive as any addiction and can wreck your soul.

Remain vigilant and aware of your needs and do everything to let other people know what your needs are. You choose if you want to find a way to make them understand your reasons. Don't be afraid you will turn out selfish; actually, try to inspire others to embrace their own needs and enjoy their power of self-improvement. This way you will all achieve better and higher quality relationships because you will all be at a higher level of self-satisfaction.

Below are additional tips on how to increase the quality of your life, leading to happier days and mastery of your emotions, self-confidence, and interaction with other people.

- Set your limits

- Don't overwork yourself. You know how much you can take on.

- Do everything to keep calm in this chaotic world.

- The quality of our activities is more important than how much we do. Your day should be fulfilled with various activities, but not the ones that will make you too exhausted in the evening.

- Moderate activity maintains optimal performance. Overuse endangers not only your body, but your mind as well.

- Make a chart: Activities you have to do. Activities you want to do. Activities you can delay. Use this chart to better organize your time and reduce stress.

Avoid multitasking. Sure, it's a great skill, but not when it exhausts you. Remember, it is quality, not quantity that counts. What are the chances you will create any good memories by doing hundred things at once? Don't feel obligated to apologize if you cannot do everything.

- Speak life over yourself.

- Believe your best is enough.

F.L.Y. Challenge Testimonial: Tachonda F. Florida

I receive many emails regarding my work and the 30-day challenge, but I never get tired of reading positive examples of change, achieving self-love, and looking at the bright side of life. It actually makes my days better. Knowing that somewhere out there is a woman who took control over her life, decided to be happy, and simply achieved it through a fun challenge gives me hope that this world can truly be a gentle place full of love and understanding.

When one person makes a positive change, to me, it is not just a confirmation of my methods; it is the first link in the chain of other positive changes. One woman can inspire another, another woman will inspire someone else, and that is how the beauty persists in this world. I am always glad to hear someone is taking these challenges seriously. Together, we build a wonderful network of happy and enlightened women. It doesn't matter who we were before or what kind of troubles were bothering us. What really matters is discovering the true core of our soul. Once we do this, we should be proud to say it out loud, just like Tachonda did.

> *"The Journey of Self-Love Challenge was one of the GREATEST things to happen to me in a long while. Latoya is so motivational, positive and inspiring, and it definitely shows in her work. Not only have I learned how to love myself and recognize my self-worth truly, but I've also learned how to say NO to anything that causes harm or negative energy in my life, how to connect on a more positive level, and how to be Happy!! Thank You for sharing*

Love Notes to Self

_____

_____

_____

_____

_____

_____

_____

_____

_____

_____

_____

_____

_____

_____

_____

_____

Love Notes to Self

_____

_____

_____

_____

_____

_____

_____

_____

_____

_____

_____

_____

_____

_____

Chapter Seven
Discover Your Fly Woman *Authority*

My Dearest Sister:

You are beautiful, unique, powerful and courageous. But, you have been to hell and back. You survived because the Creator wanted to take you on the sacred and remarkable journey of self-love. There is a calling for you to become a shining example of excellence and extraordinary self-mastery. There is a light deep within you that shines brighter than any diamond ring ever could. It is the spirit of The Creator guiding you toward total, genuine, spiritual love for who you are.

The space you might be in now – feeling broken, confused, abused, and helpless – is the perfect place for the Creator to start healing and connecting you with your essence. You will have greater appreciation for this journey and the pearls that are waiting for you at the end.

There is a great treasure at the end of your assignment of discovering and falling in love with the unique and special person you are. A sense of pride, confidence, fulfillment, and immense knowledge and understanding of self are all in store for you.

Throughout this chapter, you will use nine personal discovery passages and some questions to create what I call your Fly Woman Authority Profile. This profile will consist of all the revelations and discoveries that you will be revealed as you ponder the ideas in this chapter. This activity will also help you reflect on your character, life and belief system. This process of personal discovery will be a fun and enlightening exercise for you. As you think about your responses to some questions that you'll be presented with, you will reveal some personal truths and untapped inspiration you never knew you had. You will become connected to a very sacred and passionate part of yourself and uncover possibilities that lie deep inside your heart which will be instrumental in the process of loving yourself more deeply and authentically. These exercises will take you from the point of confusion and self-doubt to clarity and profound enlightenment.

Right now, you may be thinking: I know myself, or I don't think this part really applies to me. Well, I believe that by the end of this exercise, even if you are not convinced of it right now, you will uncover many profound aspects about yourself that might surprise you. Use the "Love Notes to Self" section at the end of this chapter to write down important revelations.

Discovery #1 What Would I Rather Be Doing?

Uncovering your life's purpose will bring you more peace. Have you allowed the need to make a living hinder you from pursuing your destiny? Do you find yourself thinking about something else you'd rather be doing other than what you are currently doing in your life? Most likely this thing that you are avoiding is something you are passionate about. As long as you continue to think you should do something else, you should. It really isn't difficult to figure out what direction you should head—listen to the spirit that lives within you. Love you enough to free yourself from the bondage of a job, relationship, or lifestyle that is not pleasing to you. Be careful not to attach to a job as your source; it is only a resource. While it is possible for the resource to become unavailable or nonexistent at some point, the source, which is your Creator has an infinite amount of resources to help meet your needs.

The need to know where your purpose lies will tug on your spirit until you are in alignment with what you are meant to do here on earth. You might not be able to change your destination immediately, but you can certainly change your direction in an instant. The first step is to discover what truly resonates with your heart and declare that you will pursue it. No matter how long it takes, you will eventually live the life you were designed to live.

A good place to start is asking yourself, what feels natural to me? When do I feel most passionate, content, and purpose-filled?

Here's how I was lead to my purpose:

Two years ago, I listened to Les Brown speeches almost every day. I hadn't quite made the connection that my purpose in life was to motivate hearts and minds, be a professional speaker, and inspire people to transform their lives and launch their businesses. All I knew was Mr. Brown's words resonated with me, and I could feel a pull for something greater in my life.

One night while I was having a hard time sleeping, a quote that Mr. Brown often recites by Carter G. Woodson played over and over in my mind, here is the quote paraphrased: *If you can determine how a person will think, you'll never have to concern yourself with what they will do. If you can make a person feel inferior, you'll never have to compel them to seek an inferior status because they'll seek it on their own. And if you can make a person feel outcasted unjustly, you'll never have to lead them to the back door; they'll go without being told. And if there is no back door, their very nature will demand one."*

As the tears rolled down my cheeks, I thought about our young people and how many of them present themselves to the world from the lowest level of consciousness, just as I had done when I was plagued with low self-esteem, a lack of self-love, and a shattered self- image. The moment I recited that quote in my mind, it was clear that my purpose was in the passion I have to encourage and uplift others. I had no idea that within a few months, I would get the opportunity to make one of the best investments in myself—to be mentored by Mr. Brown, in person.

I made two separate trips from Virginia to New York City to be a part of his Platinum Speakers Mastermind Group.

On the last day of the training, he had us all come together and join hands as he spoke to us: *"The world is waiting to receive your gift. Some people who will only respond to your voice. They will hear others speak with their ears, but when you speak, they will hear you with their hearts and their lives will forever be changed because of you."*

Today, less than two years from that date, I am humbled by the privilege of influencing the lives of thousands of people through social media, my self-love challenge, website, and various speaking engagements. I receive emails and inbox messages often from women expressing how my words help, motivate, and inspire them. This lets me know that when you focus your heart, mind, and undivided attention on something, the Creator will carve a path for you to operate in your purpose.

If you hear a call for something greater in your life, pay attention. The greatest way to honor and express love for yourself is to walk in your destiny by living your purpose with a deliberate and undying commitment. Your skills, talent, and passions are needed to help someone.

Your *job* is what you do for a living; your work is what you are living to do. Your task is to get intimately connected with yourself and the Creator so you can find your work and make it your job. This process of discovery could take some time, and you it's likely that you may not be able to uncover your purpose immediately. But, you can make a decision to put the steps in place to make measurable progress in reasonable time. With every step you take, you're closer than you were yesterday.

Discovery #2: Am I ready to make myself a priority?

You might find yourself in positions where you are tempted to put other people's needs before yours. When that time comes, don't be afraid to say no. When you say no to others, you are saying yes to yourself. Whether it's your boss or significant other, it's imperative that you recognize the importance of prioritizing your needs over the needs of others. You should say Yes to tasks that are manageable and No to those tasks that create unnecessary stress or cause you to feel overwhelmed and anxious. That's a sign that it's not in alignment with your purpose. Make it okay to say No to commitments you don't feel right about. Decide to start making your happiness, and peace of mind your priorities. Not in a selfish way, but in a holistic way that empowers and affirms you. Being sympathetic to your own needs and making the proper adjustments in your life is key to tapping inwardly for the source of true love for yourself. Remember, you can do anything, but not everything.

Sacrifice vs. Investing. One of the best things you can do for those you care about is love and take care of yourself. If you're not careful, you can become so busy doing things for your children, husband, boss, parents, and in-laws that you end up sacrificing important parts of who you are without realizing it. Don't give away all your energy and pull yourself in so many different directions trying to satisfy other people. Telling someone No and exercising your own right to be fulfilled, might create a feeling of discomfort for a while. At that moment, remain firm and stand on your decision. When you feel uneasy, it is just a sign that you are growing and stretching so far beyond the norm that your comfort zone is becoming uncomfortable. This is a natural part of the growth process. Remember that everything is hard until it gets easier.

Sacrificing yourself can cause you to become depleted while investing in yourself makes you feel worthy, energetic and progressive. Your family, career, community and the world receive a treasure when you invest in yourself and treat yourself well. When you are fulfilled, and at peace, this is the energy others will experience through you.

Discovery #3: What is my deepest desire?

Desires are not some basic interests; some are easily achievable goals or random wishes. They reside in the core of your soul. Only you can tell their nature by deep and sincere introspection. Have a little chat with your soul. Have long, relaxing conversations with your mind. Play with your desires and become friends with them. Go to a whole new level beyond sincerity.

Use these steps to help guide you:

Step one. To identify your deepest desires, go with the flow of your natural rhythm and discover the core of your inner being and your true inspiration. It should not be difficult. Although those desires are deep in your heart, they tend to become visible as you pull back the layers by asking the right questions and being honest with yourself. At this point, discovering your desires will be the most natural thing in the world.

Step two. Define what—or who—stops you from fulfilling your deepest desires. Are the obstacles so great they can make you give up? The answer should be no. Regardless of the nature of obstacles, you can win. If you can define them, you already have a greater chance of achieving them. Don't forget that sometimes the obstacle is within us. Our fears, frustrations, shy nature, and the lack of self-confidence can be a dominating group of enemies. Fighting against yourself should not be considered a battle, it is a kind of friendly negotiation, where you try to make yourself feel and be better. You will be at your best as soon as you become decisive about conquering all the inner conflicts.

Step three. Visualize your strategy. Write all the obstacles down on a piece of paper then brainstorm ideas for overcoming the obstacles. You will see that some of them are more realistic than others. Develop them in detail. If you like to write, consider capturing a story about your journey of achieving your deepest desires. Feel how easy it is to see yourself experiencing this happy ending. If you like to draw, do the same thing by drawing the image that represents your journey and expected outcomes. Once you see it on paper, you will be a step closer to seeing it in your reality. Our mind works in mysterious ways, and these little games could be helpful, not to mention they are fun and challenging as well. And could be a bit of a stress reliever (a time when "multitasking" is beneficial).

Step four. Surround yourself with people who inspire you. When you actively begin the process of achieving your deepest desires, you will discover certain people are standing in your way. There is an eternal fight between greatness and mediocrity; all you need to do is to find people who believe in your greatness above all.

Instead of focusing on people who bring you nothing but frustrations and troubles, try to focus on those people who will share positive energy with you. Even though our deepest desires are personal, we shouldn't be alone as we are trying to reach such goals. Think hard; who makes you feel good about yourself? Who gives you support? Who has the best advice for you? Who are those friends and relatives you enjoy spending time with? Who understands your needs without being judgmental? Who can you really trust? Focus on those fulfilling relationships.

This step is a matter of how well you can recognize the goodness and kindness you already have in your life. Learn how to accept a helping hand, and don't hesitate to share your paths with someone. Have you ever seen someone smile and it made you smile? Laughter is contagious, and so is positive energy. Develop the habit of searching for amazing people who will infect you with inspiration and desire to chase your dreams. Surrounding yourself with good people and light energy is the cure for many matters of the heart.

Step five. Step out of your comfort zone. At this point, you should have defined your deepest desires. You know what your obstacles are and you know who can help you. You even have a strategy. Now comes the most difficult task, which is also the task that makes you feel beyond good once you finish it—facing the real world. There is a reason we sometimes don't actualize our deepest desires. Real life sets up all kinds of barriers, and some of us don't think we are strong enough to cross them. Don't be that woman who always finds excuses to stay in her comfort zone. Do everything you can to get the inner strength necessary to go out in the world completely free.

Often times the drastic change needs to take place within us. You leave that limiting comfort zone, you will see that anything is possible. Turning desires into reality is a special kind of personal magic. As long as you have your goals in mind, this journey will be promising, with the potential to be one of the most rewarding experiences of your life. Accept the fact that you need to change everything that stops you from achieving your deepest desires.

If you are shy, you will need to develop real self-confidence. For instance, if you think that you miss out on opportunities all the time because of your meakness, you will have to find a way to become more open to new experiences. If your thoughts tend to be negative, you will have to find the light in your life. It is difficult, but it is far from impossible, and when you manage to deal with those difficulties, you will achieve those deepest desires. You will know the sweet taste of fulfilled goals. You will fly!

Discovery #4: What inspires me?

Motivation is the unique bundle of your emotions that drive you through life; while your goals and inspiration are your best friends on the road to personal discovery. Without motivation and inspiration, we wouldn't have any ambitions and life would be pointless. Unfortunately, we are rarely aware of our inspiration or motivation, which is why you have to think about them actively.

You know those "spot the difference" games? In these games, you are given two images that resemble one another. Your task is to spot the subtle differences between the two. Imagine two similar images representing your life. One should be the image of your average life, while the other one should represent the best of you. The difference between those two images is your tenacity: the ability to wake up the inspiration in you and the ability to motivate yourself to move forward.

What inspires you to focus and accelerate to reach your goals? Is it slow music on the radio while you do things you love? Is it the warmth of your family's home? It might be a book you enjoy reading. It can be something seemingly insignificant to the world, but important to you. Maybe you are inspired by nature, or little things give you the greatest ideas. Also, don't forget all the amazing people who can inspire you.

It is important to be aware of your inspiration, so you can easily find it when you need it. It is also important to be sincere when you think about why you are inspired to do something. Inspiration is the cherry on top of the cake, and the why is the first layer. Nothing is possible if the base is wrong. Sincerely answering this question might be the key to unlocking every door in your life.

The answer can be complex or as simple as I'm inspired when I know I'm making a difference, which is legitimate. Having no answer is concerning. It could be a sign that you don't really know yourself yet.

Even if you haven't thought about where your inspiration lies, it is not too late to start the discovery process. It is your responsibility to yourself to know what inspires and motivates you so you can keep it close by. It's important to know why you want to do something because you will then have clearer direction when it comes to executing.

Discovery #5: What makes me angry?

The word angry seems to be charged with negative energy and bitterness, but there are many layers of anger, and some of them are helpful. Some anger might fuel you to make a great impact. We are angry when we see certain kinds of injustice. We are angry when we know people exploit others. This kind of anger moves us. We want to use or influence problem-solving skills to make an impact. This type of anger turned to passion reminds me of a quote by Mahatma Gandhi who once said, "Be the change you want to see."

You don't have to feel obligated to save the world and solve the toughest problems of humanity. Even if some things make us angry, sometimes they are beyond our reach. However, there are many problems you can solve, from the ones related to your intimate circle of people to the ones regarding your community. There are many chances to contribute to some of the world's most pressing problems. If poverty is what makes you angry, you can participate in numerous charities or start an annual food drive of your own. Always remember that it's possible to transform anger into solutions.

Discovery #6: Did I pause to celebrate my last accomplishment big or small?

We have goals and we have ideas about the best ways to achieve them. We have our accomplishments, but often we miss out on the satisfaction of being praised for a great job. Society constantly imposes rules and demands, our time is precious, and we shouldn't waste a second doing something unproductive. Sometimes those unwritten rules manage to make us feel anxious when there is no reasonable explanation for it. Time isn't all about productivity. It's also about enjoying the results of our productivity. Show some appreciation for yourself and dare to enjoy the moment you've worked so diligently to manifest. Where is the joy and fulfillment of your accomplishment if you cannot stop and celebrate the moment?

If you worked hard and gave your all to something, you deserve to get the maximum satisfaction from your accomplishments, and in turn, acknowledge your time was worth all the hard work. Tis appreciation can boost your desires to become even better. The joy of celebration could be your personal motivation for further plans and goals. Go ahead and reward yourself. Spend time doing only things you like. Take a trip or buy something you really want. Take a bubble bath, read a book, or just have a long walk. Play some music you love. Eat something you haven't had for a long time and forget the calories.

Of course, don't forget all the people who are a part of your success. Let them be a part of your celebration as well. In a nutshell, your accomplishments deserve proper reward; celebrations make you remember how beautiful it is to be alive, to have goals, turning them into reality, and seeing them realized.

Discovery#7 What are my greatest strengths?

First of all, everyone has many talents and strengths, but it can be difficult to determine what makes you strong, if we are talking about artistic talents—singing, drawing, writing—that's usually obvious as those talents are often displayed in childhood.

Still, it's possible to have artistic strengths and not even know it.

Have you tried painting or sculpting? What about knitting, creating unique jewelry, or making postcards? Art is a wide field of various and interesting activities. Some of them may be your ideal hobby or even a profession. You cannot know you are good at something if you don't try it.

Being open to new experiences and having a healthy curiosity is the key to self-discovery. Art is just one example. There are several other strengths that you might possess. But the principle is the same. Your strength can be anything you know and love to do. All you have to do is practice it and sharpen your knowledge and expertise in that area.

Maybe you think it takes too much effort and time to randomly discover aspects of your purpose and destiny. Yes, it does take time, but who said this journey should be random? Focus on those things you love. If you are into art, try several artistic activities. If you are into writing, read a lot and try to find the best literary form to express yourself. If you are into helping people, think about all the things you can offer them. Maybe what you have to offer is compassion and good advice. Some of us are great listeners, which is a real skill and should not be underestimated. Many of our greatest gifts are intangible.

The key to your treasure chest full of gifts from the Creator lies within you. Everything starts with you. Sometimes discovering your gifts is a matter of getting connecting with the best parts of who you are and those things that come naturally to. Be careful not to dismiss even the smallest attributes. Every talent matters, no matter how small or insignificant it seems. If it makes you feel fulfilled, cherish it and figure out how to implement it.

Discovery #8 What do I want to do for humanity?

You have probably asked yourself what this world would look like if things were different. Big news: this world can be different, and you can change it. It is easy to say one person cannot change the world, but history has proven this theory wrong—many times. What if Edison gave up on working with electricity? What if Bell never tried to make a telephone? The desire to change the world is a normal and natural human experience. Unfortunately, neglecting such desires is also a common human habit. Many people have allowed their ideas to die with them. Make up your mind that this will not happen to you.

Challenge the spirit of complacency. You are a woman capable of achieving so much greatness. You can change the world! Once you feel completely comfortable with the woman you are and define and accept your strengths and talents. Once you get in touch with your true self, changing the world will be a joyful task for you. Of course, you have to think about it really hard and define what your contribution to humanity will be, but in reality, your options are endless.

Changing the world doesn't necessarily mean that you need to do something amazing and never before seen. You can always find a way to make an impact in your local community. Maybe you can volunteer to help elderly or homeless people. You can organize cultural, sports, or kids events in your neighborhood to keep the place alive—who knows, maybe it will become a tradition.

Have strong faith in your abilities. Be self-confident about things you believe in and remind yourself why they matter to you and humankind. You are not alone in this essential battle. Inspire others to join you, realize change is not impossible, but inevitable. Bond with people around you, feel their needs, and the needs of humanity through them. Relate those needs to your strengths and desires, and you are on the path of your destiny.

Discovery #9 Who am I really?

This question is philosophical, psychological, existential, and metaphysical—and probably the most difficult question you will ever have to answer. There is no right or wrong answer on this life test.

However, not all the answers are satisfying. Some answers

feel right, while others feel wrong. Here is a hint: sincere answers should always feel right. Every other important step you take on your journey to true self-love depends on your sincerity while you are dealing with this bittersweet question. You need to know who you are in order to make a big change in your life. You need to know your true nature if you would like to influence the nature of the world.

Discovering who you are requires deep focus. It is not enough if you say your name, education, profession, and social roles. You should forget about those descriptions. They are often repressive and create limitations. We are not defined by our names and jobs—at least we shouldn't be. So, forget about your life's roles and attributes given by birth. Also, forget about other's opinions. People tend to project their limiting beliefs and jaded views on others. As FLY Women, you should be immune to such prejudices when you interact with people. Remember, the question wasn't: "Who am I really, according to other people's opinion, but who am I really."

Getting the answer requires self-reflection. Be your own mirror. Look into your past, present, and future. Emphasize your feelings. Eliminate the labels society has branded you with. Embrace what you think is important as an unrestricted emancipated, and unique woman. Get to the very core of your being and think about what makes you special, identify your most prominent personality traits. Maybe your sincerity will acknowledge some negative traits. Don't worry. As long as you are true to yourself, you have answered this question successfully. If you become aware, you are not the person you want to be—at least not yet—you are making a huge step towards changes. Remember, before you can change, you must become aware a change is needed. You reading this book indicates you're on the right path.

FLY Woman Authority Recap

We learn about ourselves in many ways: through new situations, new relationships, our mistakes or successes, hobbies, and many other activities. Our experiences tell our story. We learn about ourselves as we walk in the park and admire flowers.

We also learn about ourselves as we weep after a loss of a loved one and wonder if we expressed our love to the fullest.

Simply said, we learn as we live. However, sometimes we don't think about those life lessons consciously; we are simply not focused enough to learn from what we do. The Fly Woman Authority exercise will enable you to reflect more deeply on who you are as you travel this journey of life and love.

Journey to Self-Love Challenge Testimonial: Tamisha Taylor-Renrick

One of the most important factors that have contributed to the success of The Journey to Self-Love Challenge is that it was meant to help women focus on themselves. I wanted to wake up the participants' minds and souls, make them really think about their life's journeys and help them improve the quality of their days. Since self- love, and self-reflection are serious issues, I really wanted to make things easier and more fun. From my experience with many women, I can say they enjoy fun little games and challenges that finally lead to higher cognition. That is why I have made many different tasks, challenging ideas, and suggestions. I also love the step-by-step concept; it seems much easier to complete challenges when they are presented in that form. Just like we naturally walk step-by-step, we should also learn about ourselves step-by-step. I wasn't sure how this challenge would turn out; the theory is one thing, while reality is often much different. But I had strong faith that I had created something meaningful.

Tamisha is another FLY Woman who shared her story about my program, and I'm glad I can share those sweet words with you:

> *I am learning more about myself than I*
> *thought possible. I believed that I had a grasp*
> *on myself, my goals, and my past. Self-*
> *reflection changes a lot of things. Taking time*
> *alone with myself, I now see that there were*
> *areas of me that I was leaving untouched.*
> *Thank you, Latoya, for creating this*
> *challenge. Thank you for challenging me to*
> *learn myself!*

Love Notes to Self

Love Notes to Self

_____

_____

_____

_____

_____

_____

_____

_____

_____

_____

_____

_____

_____

_____

Chapter Eight
The Self-Love Victory
is Yours

My Dearest Sister:

*Affirmations alone will not be enough to get
you through the most trying times.
Repeating empty words won't do it. You'll
need to strengthen your belief in yourself.
Truly believing in what you're saying is
what will make the difference. What do you
believe is possible for your life?*

*Who do you believe you can become? Do you
believe you are capable and tenacious? Can
you say with conviction that you are
resilient and courageous? Fortify your
belief! Speak life over yourself from the
depths of who you are, and your belief will
hold you up. Repeat affirmations, and think
positively, but remember that it's more
important to really believe.*

In this chapter, I will speak to you in affirmation. I will refer to you in this chapter as though you have already mastered the practice of self-love and as if you are a shining example of what it means to possess a genuine affinity for one's self. Everyone enters the world in an own unique and authentic state, but most people end up as imitations of other people. There are so many people in the world who think alike, dress alike, and behave alike that it's hard to find an authentic person in a crowd.

When you manifest true love for yourself and decide to operate authentically as who you are, you can no longer be a variation of someone else. Your uniqueness will be a reflection of your spirit, character, and the confidence of knowing and loving who you are. As long as the world has been in existence, and as long as it continues to exist, there will never be another you. Appreciate that you are exclusive, and express yourself from the depths of your being. Get connected to the purpose that the Creator has for your life. Your destiny and your path are different from everyone else around you.

You are a Masterpiece

While many people struggle for a long time to discover a sense of self- worth and personal achievement for their lives, you recognize and understand your value and significance comes from the Creator who made you in His image. You pursue life with confidence so that you can live out the purpose for your life. You are courageous, determined, and not afraid to step outside your comfort zone. You know that you have a Divine purpose, and your confidence, ambition, and faith will keep you motivated and excited about your life.

You don't spend time contemplating whether what you're doing is going to work. You proceed with certainty because you have a mission to pursue. You are confident in your natural abilities, and you know your strengths. Life's experiences have taught you to be resilient and relentless, so when you fail at something, you get back up and start again and again until you get the result you want. You know if you keep going you will succeed.

You look at failure as a unique learning experience that provides wisdom and guidance on what you need to do differently going forward. Quitting is never an option for you.

Also, you understand the authority and power that you have to manifest what you want through your thoughts and language. Therefore, you monitor what you see and hear. You are also mindful of the conversations you entertain. You keep your mind focused on your goals, and you keep distractions to a minimum. You believe that all the resources and tools you need to be successful will manifest as a result of your intense and unmovable focus on what you're destined to achieve. You adopt new and rewarding disciplines and habits such as reading, praying, meditating, and journaling to strengthen your character and build mental fortitude.

There is no Such Thing As Competition For You

You have connected with your individuality, and you are now comfortable with the process of loving and accepting yourself. You are a one of a kind designer's original. No one could ever be you.

Therefore, others do not intimidate you. No one can threaten your value or your personal power—although they may try. But you do not seek to outdo them; you are simply yourself. You refuse to entertain the thought that you have to compete with others to be validated. You have also learned that it is not your assignment to try and conform others to your way. You realize you can inspire people, but to be changed, they must seek the Creator's wisdom.

Honoring this perspective compels you to mind your own business and avoid internalizing other people's issues. There is a fine line between confidence and arrogance, and you are wise enough to know the difference.

You realize that when you operate in truth, this is a reflection of your confidence, but if you belittle others for doing what feels right for them and try to manipulate them into adjusting to and walking your path, the line to arrogance has been crossed. You don't seek to boost your ego or exalt yourself by putting other people down. You know the importance of rising to your own personal potential, and you are aware that all you're competing at is to be better than you were the day before.

Because you know who you are, and you appreciate and love yourself, you never weigh your progress against what other people do or have done. You realize that your process is supposed to be different from everyone else's, and the way your journey unfolds has nothing to do with anyone else, as long as you stay true to who you are. You are also open to learning new skills and ideas from other people who have gifts and talents you admire. You are also open-minded enough to accept mentorship as a way to enhance yourself, not as a way to mimic or emulate other people.

You appreciate the value that learning from others can offer, but your style, focus, and goals remain your own. As you live according to your own FLY woman authority, you are experiencing the gratification that comes from serving the world through your own natural gifts and purpose. Your life has a sense of meaning, and you use your time, talents, experience, and energy in the most productive and fruitful ways possible.

You Are Free from Jealousy

Your personal dominion has fortified your confidence so much that you don't feel jealous or envious when you see people doing well. When other people can do things better than you can, it doesn't make you feel less than or beneath anyone. You realize we all have been blessed with our own personal skills and gifts that are an expression of who we are as individuals. There are things you do better than others. You appreciate that fact that we have been designed in such a way that and all of our gifts in some way complement each other. Therefore, you know that no one has anything greater than you have, because the skills and gifts you have, were given to you specifically. You know that jealousy is a reflection of low self-worth and diminished self-love, and you do not lack in either area. You realize that being jealous because someone else was born to do something that you weren't, does not serve you in any way. Your focus is always on using your own skills and talents to live the best most rewarding life possible.

You Turned Your Fears into Faith

Having discovered your purpose has provided you assurance about your journey. You have learned to turn fear into faith to stay in a peaceful state of mind. As a result of his shift, your attitude is one that represents limitlessness. You put your energy into manifesting the things you want, and you are mindful about keeping your language in alignment with what you believe is possible. Even when life throws you curve balls, and the struggles and hardships show up, you are resilient and composed. You don't waste time worrying about situations you cannot change. You have adopted new disciplines which help you stay optimistic about the future and keep your faith strong.

Through personal development and reflection, you have discovered that fear is merely a false illusion. As the late Zig Ziglar so precisely stated, "Fear is only **f**alse **e**vidence **a**ppearing **r**eal." You have made up in your mind not to feed fear but to starve it. You realize you have the power to dismiss thoughts of fear and inadequacy.

Challenging yourself to do things that stretch you and make you uncomfortable has helped you to see beyond your comfort zone. You know that as long as you push fear away, deny, or ignore it, you will be held captive by it much longer than if you face and overcome it. So when you experience the fear of doing something new or challenging, you face your fears and do it anyway.

Prayer, positive affirmations, meditation, and positive self-talk are all a part of your daily self-love enhancers. There is supernatural power in these rituals. If you choose to direct your consistent focus toward the principles of self-love actions that I have laid out in this book and work on them, you will begin to accept and love yourself more. Just imagine how much you'll appreciate you when you exercise many of the disciplines, tips and rituals of self-love. It is true that you can only love a person as much as you love yourself. The more self-love you have for yourself, the better prepared you are for healthy relationships, increased happiness, personal mastery. And so many other gratifying experiences. Even more, you will start to attract people and circumstances to you that support your well-being. This is your divine time to FLY!

Journey to Self-Love Challenge Testimonial: Darlene Young

Darlene Young was crippled in the area of self-love before accepting the calling. She put her heart and soul's need second to the needs of others. Here's her testimony:

> Since I accepted "The Journey to Self- Love Challenge," I can honestly say, I have learned the meaning of (F)irst(L)ove(Y)ourself. When I began the challenge, I had many personal barriers before me which restricted me and stifled my personal development. In the midst of my last trial, I learned about The Journey to Self-Love Challenge Facebook community. Connecting with Latoya and the other FLY sisters gave me faith to believe I was worthy of the Journey to love myself. I needed the support and extra push. I have always been a nurturer, problem solver, and the go to person. I had a poor habit of putting my needs last. When I accepted the self-love challenge, I learned to love me as I love those I'm trying to help. The daily audio affirmations were the perfect reinforcement as I listened to them in my car daily.

Love Notes to Self

Love Notes to Self

_____

_____

_____

_____

_____

_____

_____

_____

_____

_____

_____

_____

_____

_____

_____

_____

_____

_____

ABOUT THE AUTHOR

Latoya Johnson is a motivational speaker and success coach. She's the mother of two beautiful, intelligent children, ages twelve and nine. Latoya grew up in foster care and suffered from low self-esteem and a lack of self-love for many years. As a lost teen and young adult, she looked for love in all the wrong places and was involved in many self- sabotaging behaviors. After many tough lessons and a decision to take accountability for her life and future, Latoya set her life in a new direction. Through self-reflecting and many years of strategic personal development, Latoya has been groomed into a highly sought after self-love advisor and business coach.

As a respected social media personality, Latoya encourages women to love themselves with authenticity, without apology and coaches them to launch their business strategically. Latoya also educates youth in the area of finances and wealth building.

She is the owner of Defining Your Destiny LLC, which includes three legs, FLY (First Love Yourself) University, Fly (First Launch Your) Business Coaching and Fly (Financially Literate Young) Leaders. Latoya is also founder of The Journey to Self-Love Challenge, an online Face Book community of over eleven thousand women.

Latoya is honored to have been personally coached by Les Brown.